Behind the Silhouettes

EXPLORING THE MYTHS OF CHILD SEXUAL ABUSE

Olive Travers

with Sylvia Thompson

THE
BLACKSTAFF
PRESS

BELFAST

First published in 1999 by
The Blackstaff Press Limited
3 Galway Park, Dundonald, Belfast BT16 2AN, Northern Ireland

© Olive Travers, 1999
All rights reserved

Typeset by Techniset Typesetters, Newton-le-Willows, Merseyside

Printed in Ireland by ColourBooks Limited

A CIP catalogue record for this book
is available from the British Library

ISBN 0-85640-634-1

OLIVE TRAVERS is a native of Country Fermanagh. She has a B.Ed
from St Mary's College of Education, Belfast, and worked as a teacher
for five years before returning to university to study psychology
at the University of Ulster and Queen's University Belfast. In the
mid-1980s, while working as a community care psychologist in

For Dr Tim McBride, who has so generously shared his lifetime of professional expertise and whose non-judgemental wisdom and compassion has greatly influenced those who have had the privilege of working with him.

Contents

Acknowledgements

I would like to thank Michael McGinley and the North-Western Health Board for their support and assistance to me in the writing of this book.

Thank you to Sylvia Thompson, whose collaboration and help has been invaluable in bringing to a wider audience the knowledge available from research in the area of sex abuse.

I would like especially to thank Dr Tim McBride, Consultant Pyschiatrist, without whose help this book would not have been possible. He brought to his pioneering group treatment for sex offenders in the 1980s his unique blend of humanity and professional expertise, including his experience of setting up residential treatment programmes for alcoholics in the 1970s. His belief, that working with sex offenders contributes significantly to the protection of children, bolstered the treatment team during times in the past twelve years when there was little general recognition of the value of the work that we do.

I would like to acknowledge the contribution of my colleagues on the treatment team. They include: Hugh McFadden, Barry Ramsay, Jon Stack and Seamus Gordon from the North-Western Health Board, and Paula Cooney, Mildred Gilmore and Josephine Devine from the Probation and Welfare Service of the Department of Justice.

Thank you also to Dr Ann Moriarty, Queen's University Belfast, and Mary Brown, Western Health and Social Services Board, Omagh, County Tyrone, for their advice and support.

Last, but not least, I would like to thank my husband Anthony for his patience and encouragement, and my four precious children, Ailbhe, Kate, Eoin and Eamon Ross, who have been my inspiration, because it is for them and for all children that we have the responsibility to make this world a safer place.

Foreword

Over the past twenty years, child sexual abuse has become a much discussed topic. It is a complex and emotive subject which challenges our most deep-rooted fears and beliefs. The present situation where an increasing number of children are being taken into care because they are defined to be at risk, coupled with the expressed need for more prison spaces and more resources for protecting children, is clearly not fully addressing the problem.

Child abuse, like alcohol abuse, affects the whole family. It forces each family member to take sides, and by and large the current practices do not cope adequately with the various difficulties that such abuse brings in its wake. By looking at child sex abuse in all its complexities in this book, Olive Travers takes us much closer to the core issues and dilemmas that confront us as a society when honestly attempting to understand and deal with the many faces of child sexual abuse.

Through my work as a psychiatrist encountering both sex

offenders and the victims of child sexual abuse, I have come to realise that many of the quick-fix solutions proposed by politicians and social commentators do not reflect the answers called for in practice.

Contrary to popular opinion, many victims of child sexual abuse have no desire for revenge. They do, however, want an apology from the abuser which acknowledges his/her responsibility for the abuse. Many victims feel aggrieved that they were not listened to or heard when they first tried to tell someone about their experience of abuse. Then, often, when their case is brought to public attention, their own personal needs are not adequately taken on board. Many also find that the media coverage of child sexual abuse – in all its sordid detail and lack of respect for the individuals involved – discourages the further disclosure of sexual abuse by other victims.

Also contrary to popular belief, child abuse is not necessarily about sexual activity. It is primarily about control, dominance and the abuse of power. Sex offenders are not a single group of individuals who are inherently evil and manipulative. True, some are but others are maladjusted people who seek an inappropriate closeness with children or whose immature attempt to cope with loneliness results in child sexual abuse. Others have themselves been sexually abused as children. While this is no excuse for their behaviour, it does pose questions regarding the different and often opposing views we hold of victims and offenders.

As Olive Travers proposes here, we must look carefully for real solutions which will reduce the crime of child sexual abuse in our society. To do so, we must develop a working model from the very hopeful research which shows that after treatment, the relapse rate of sex offenders is much reduced as compared with offenders who are not treated (8.5 per cent as opposed to 35 per cent). We must also accept that all abusers and victims are not the same and learn to deal with each case in all its individual complexity. As responsible members of society, we must search within ourselves to truly understand the complexities of child sexual abuse and reach for genuine preventative measures to reduce its prevalence. This book takes some bold steps forward to help us do so.

TIM McBRIDE

CONSULTANT PSYCHIATRIST

ST CONAL'S HOSPITAL, LETTERKENNY,

COUNTY DONEGAL

January 1999

Introduction
Coming to terms with the issues around sexual abuse

Child sexual abuse has always occurred in spite of an almost universal taboo. The origins of the taboo lie in biology and in the recognition that the prevention of parent/child sexual relationships is necessary for the healthy emotional and psychological development of the child. The only exceptions made were the acceptance in the past of royal incest and incest as part of magical or satanic rituals. However, we now know that the taboo has failed to prevent countless children throughout the years from being sexually abused, not only by immediate family members, but by adults outside the family.

Offences range from sexual fondling and touching to masturbation, anal/vaginal rape, voyeurism or making a child watch sexual acts or pornography, to urinating/defecating on a child, abuse with animals, anal/vaginal penetration with an object or abuse in the context of occult rituals.

The fact that the emotional, physical and sexual abuse of children has always been with us does not appear to make it any easier for the general public to come to terms with its existence. Indeed, many professionals have had great difficulty in accepting the existence of the sexual abuse of children. Unlike physical abuse, sexual abuse may not result in injuries which can be easily observed.

Public and professional disbelief regarding the existence of sexual abuse is, however, influenced less by this lack of physical evidence than by the myths within which sexual abuse has remained shrouded.

In 1886 Sigmund Freud identified the damage caused by sexual abuse in his adult patients in the statement, 'I put forward the thesis that at the bottom of every hysteria, there are one or more occurrences of premature sexual experience . . . belonging to the earliest years of childhood.'

Had he stuck to his beliefs that child sexual abuse was commonplace and that it caused emotional illness in many of its victims, he would have changed the course of history in terms of the recognition of such abuse. However, Freud was before his time and he was unable to withstand the scorn and censure which his claims attracted both from his colleagues and from society in general. He then retracted his theory that childhood sexual abuse resulted in mental illness, and put in its place a theory that the female accounts of sexual abuse perpetrated on them by their fathers were fantasies based on each woman's unconscious desire to have sex with her father.[1] So the clock was set back by about one hundred years, and the myth was established that childhood reporting of sexual abuse reflected a projection of the child's wish for possessive control over the parent. The girl was viewed as seeing herself as her mother's rival for her father's love in this Electra complex, the Freudian female complex corresponding to the Oedipus complex (which involves the unconscious wish of the boy to eliminate his father and be alone with his mother).

The existence of the physical abuse of children gained

recognition only between the mid-1960s and the mid-1970s in Britain. It was only after society accepted the widespread incidence of physical abuse of children (and put in place measures to try to deal with it) that the damage done to children by emotional abuse and deprivation was considered. The acknowledgement of the existence of sexual abuse then occurred within this context.[2]

In Ireland, it was only in the early to mid-1970s that a version of the welfare state emerged (which had done so much to promote the protection of children in Britain). The statutory health services began to employ greater numbers of social workers in childcare. Major social changes since the 1960s, in particular the impact of mass unemployment, were seen to have given the state a wider role in this area.[3] In conjunction with this, the work of the Women's Movement highlighted the existence of child sexual abuse, which has been described as 'a massive societal black spot'.[4]

In the 1990s the ignorance and silence surrounding this issue were further challenged.[5] A number of high-profile child abuse cases, both physical and sexual, have focused public and media attention on the problem. The 'X case' in 1992, the Kilkenny incest case in 1993, the tragic death of Kelly Fitzgerald, the Fr Brendan Smyth case in 1994, the McColgan case in 1998, and the disclosures of the abuse of children in the care of the Goldenbridge Orphanage and Madonna House in 1997 all combined with numerous other exposures of abuse by priests, careworkers and family members to provide irrefutable evidence of the grimness of many children's lives.

Child sexual abuse emerged as a complex and emotionally charged area of public concern. Disclosures of sordid aspects of human behaviour have had a dramatic and wide-ranging impact on the political system and the Catholic church. Disquiet about the handling of one case alone, that of Fr Brendan Smyth, resulted in political upheaval involving a change of government in the Republic of Ireland, the resignation of an attorney-general, and, within the Catholic church, the resignation of an abbot.

Researchers have identified a process which the media, the public and professionals go through to come to terms with child abuse and neglect.[6] The first stage of this process is called the 'Denial and Minimisation' stage (which was the norm in Ireland before the mid-1980s). What happens here is that although cases of abuse are identified, they are seldom reported in the media. If they are, they are seen as bizarre incidents which have no meaning in ordinary life. There is a 'shoot the messenger' reaction. People who try to bring the problem to public attention, such as those involved in the Women's Movement, are often themselves attacked and have improper motives imputed to them.

This Denial response is all about not wanting to know ugly facts which destroy a comfortable image of society and raise disturbing personal questions. Typical denial responses are: 'It can't be true', 'It's exaggerated', 'These women are all lesbians/manhaters anyway', 'This wouldn't happen in Ireland' and 'No one I know would do such a thing.'

The Denial stage can be sustained for a surprisingly long time, as is witnessed by the number of people who remained in this stage for over ten years after sexual abuse became a topical issue. However, as the reporting of abuse continues to increase and evidence of its prevalence builds, most people reach a stage where denial is no longer possible.

At this point, it is often replaced by a stage characterised by anger and a desire to punish. Here, 'Lock them up and throw away the key' or 'Castrate them' are two familiar 'anger' reactions against those who sexually abuse children. Other reactions are more extreme, as typified by the outburst of a Dublin taxi driver when he heard that I was going to a conference on child abuse: 'Them bastards should be castrated – no, that would be too good for them, they should then get a bullet in the spine and spend the rest of their days in a wheelchair; then they'd never touch another child again.' That moment did not seem a good time to express my beliefs about the benefits of treatment for sex offenders.

Public anger can also be directed at the systems which fail to discover abuse, or which are seen to cover it up. Thus we saw in Ireland the outrage provoked by the notorious 'Kilkenny case', where a father's sadistic physical and sexual abuse of his daughter went undetected for years in spite of numerous agencies being involved with the family. This resulted in a public inquiry, both to appease this anger and to provide guidelines to prevent repetition of the mistakes made. In Belgium, the horrific child murders of Marc Dutroux and his accomplices led to mass street demonstrations by a disillusioned public who felt that they could no longer trust those in authority.

In spite of all the anger expressed, however, there remains a tendency to isolate the situation and the perpetrator by presenting them as being 'extraordinary'. This second stage in the process of coming to terms with abuse is labelled the 'Anger and Isolation' stage. Terms such as 'monster' and 'evil' are used to describe the abusers. They are all perceived to be of the same class, and this and other distinctions are used to create distance.

Medicalisation is another type of isolation which belongs to this stage. The sexual abuse of children is seen as the province of the doctors who deal with the sick, the strange and the perverted. Sexual abuse can therefore be placed beyond ordinary experience.

Remedies which are proposed at this stage focus on punishment, frequently of an extreme kind, such as that advocated by the Dublin taxi driver. This response acts as a kind of exorcism. The pervasiveness of the problem and its origins in human behaviour and social conditions are still denied. Television talk shows and documentaries raise awareness of the existence of abuse but rarely move beyond outrage to the next stage of coming to terms with sexual abuse.

This third stage in the process is identified as 'Despair and Ennui'. Here, it is recognised that the sexual abuse of children is widespread and that it is not confined to a particular section of the population or the result of inexplicable external forces. As more and more cases are reported, it becomes apparent that simple remedies involving punishment or threats are not working. People who have had only a passing interest give up expecting anything worthwhile to come out of their indignation. Others, while recognising that abuse does exist, believe that it is not their responsibility. It comes to be accepted that the sexual abuse of children is an unfortunate fact of life. Those who are abusing or who have abused their children find their rationalisations or 'twisted thinking' unchallenged unless the law is involved.

People who work with affected groups, both victims and abusers, cannot sustain the fatalism of the Despair and Ennui stage for long. Service providers and voluntary workers, as well as victims, family members and neighbours, grow frustrated at not being heard and supported by the public and the authorities.

The final stage in the process of coming to terms with sexual abuse is the 'Engagement' stage. True Engagement with the problem of child abuse comes with the realisation that it is widespread and that it is linked to our way of life and attitudes as well as to individual characteristics. Accompanying this realisation is the desire among concerned people to do something effective to reduce it.

I view myself as having reached this Engagement stage through my work with both the victims and the perpetrators of sex abuse for over twelve years. This book arises in part out of my frustration with the public and the media at not moving on from the shocked, angry stage of dealing with sexual abuse.

There remains a predominantly reductionist, simplistic portrayal of sexual abuse by all strands of the media, the legal system and many professionals working in the area. In addition, the sensationalism and hostility associated with high-profile cases serve only to trivialise a serious problem and to delay the development of a community approach in which everyone will have a part to play and which will provide for victims and perpetrators according to their needs.

In this book, my aim is to go beyond the simple reactionary solutions to child sex abuse and look deeper into the human psyche at this complex problem. Through an honest and thorough analysis of all the dimensions of the sexual abuse of children, I come to the conclusion that we, as a society, must engage in this problem – sincerely and wholeheartedly. Only by doing so can we prevent its occurrence where possible and above all protect our children from such experiences. I hope you, the readers, will gain some useful insight and understanding from my efforts.

Please note that while 'she' is used predominantly throughout the book to refer to victims of sexual abuse, and 'he' to refer to abusers, this does not imply that boys are not victims, or that women do not abuse. Also, to protect the identities of abusers and their victims, names have been changed, case histories have been disguised and composite case histories have been used in most instances.

OLIVE TRAVERS
COUNTY DONEGAL
January 1999

1

Childhood experiences of sexual abuse
Why many children never reveal their hidden secret

There is a dangerous assumption among the general public that if children are being sexually abused, they will always be able to tell someone. When children do not tell on the abuser, they are then seen either not to be damaged by the abuse or to be, in some way, actively responsible for it.

In this chapter, I will survey the different types of sexual abuse and how an abuser creates the abusive relationship with the child. I will also look at children's confusion and powerlessness in such situations as well as the various ways in which they learn to cope with being sexually abused. Finally, on a more optimistic note, I will discuss how a more open social context can and does reduce the trauma of sexual abuse.

I believe it cannot be overemphasised that no child is ever

responsible for being sexually abused. Children are incapable of giving their consent to sexual activity with adults because they are unable to understand what it is they are giving their consent to. The child does not have the power to refuse to participate. The unequal distribution of power between abuser and abused throws the full weight of responsibility on the adult involved. The large numbers of adult victims of child sexual abuse who in the past decade have reported their abuse for the first time is testimony to the fact that many children do not tell anyone when they are being sexually abused. This inability to tell another adult what is happening to them is one of the real horrors of sexual abuse.

One of the difficulties many children, teenagers and even adults have in revealing the abuse is their confusion as to whether what happened to them was indeed sexual abuse. The range of activities which are considered to be sexually abusive is very large. In the UK Department of Health document *Working Together under the Children Act 1989*, child sexual abuse is defined as 'actual or likely exploitation of a child or adolescent. The child may be dependent and/or developmentally immature.'

In the Republic of Ireland Department of Health procedures for the notification of suspected child abuse between the Health Boards and the police or *gardaí* (1995), sexual abuse is defined as 'the use of children by others for sexual gratification. This can take many forms, and includes rape and other sexual assaults, allowing children to view sexual acts, or to be exposed to, or involved in, pornography, exhibitionism, and other perverse acts.' Sexual abuse can, however, be divided into two main categories – non-contact sexual abuse and contact sexual abuse.[1]

Non-contact sexual abuse includes:

- age-inappropriate sexual comments made to a child. This includes obscene phone calls.

- exhibitionism, i.e. when an adult exposes his/her genitals to a child.

- voyeurism, i.e. when an adult observes a child in a sexual manner when he/she is undressing, taking a bath or using the toilet. This also includes exposing children to pornographic pictures, videotapes or films.

The intent of the adult is what determines when these non-contact behaviours are sexually abusive. Activities such as exhibitionism or voyeurism may be difficult to label as intrusive within a family context. Basically, if the end goal of the activity is the sexual gratification of the adult, even when there is no sexual activity between the adult and the child, the behaviour is abusive. The intent behind the non-contact behaviour is also often to desensitise the child and is part of the 'grooming' process which leads up to contact sexual abuse.

Contact sexual abuse includes:

- intimate kissing of the child on the mouth or kissing the child's breasts or genitals
- handling or fondling in which the adult touches, caresses or rubs the child's genitals or breasts or has the child touch the adult's body in the same way
- fellatio or cunnilingus in which the child is forced to have oral-genital contact with the adult or when an adult has oral-genital contact with the child
- vaginal or anal intercourse, when an adult penetrates the child's vagina or anus with a finger, penis or other object or when the adult forces the child to penetrate the adult with a finger, penis or other object
- frottage, when the adult rubs him/herself against the child in a sexual manner
- pornography – taking pictures or making videos or films of children performing sexual acts with one another or with adults or animals

The so-called 'grooming' of the child mentioned above is often the way the adult abuser manipulates the child into taking part in sexual activities. This is often a long and subtle process in which secrecy plays a large part. Abusers are usually pleasant people who are attractive and non-threatening to the child. Giving the child extra attention, buying her sweets and gifts, asking the child to help with jobs, playing rough-and-tumble games are all part of this subtle 'grooming' process. It is often in this way that the abuser then progresses from non-contact abuse to the more serious, contact abuse. 'Clever' abusers will be very careful to make sure that their activities with the child are kept secret so that they can continue the abuse indefinitely.

Most sexual abuse occurs within the context of an established relationship between the abuser and child.[2] Family members who abuse usually have less 'grooming' to do because they already have a relationship with the child. It is also sometimes easier for a neighbour, friend or babysitter to nurture a relationship with a child with the intention of sexually abusing her because of their particular proximity to the child and their status as a trusted person within the family.

In such circumstances, the abuse is often explained away as something which happens to all children. The child is thus manipulated and enmeshed into a relationship in which the sexual abuse is just one part. Precisely because the abuser is most often a loved and trusted person in the child's life, it is easy to persuade the child to keep 'our little secret'. The child may also be given special treats, sweets, money and presents as rewards for keeping the secret.

The psychological coercion of the victim may become more sinister if the abuser becomes anxious about being discovered. The child may be openly threatened with punishment for telling or, more deviously, given responsibility for the abuse and the consequences of telling. The abuser may tell the child that she will be taken away, locked up, et cetera if she tells, as it is all her fault. Alternatively, the threat may be used of the loved family member being taken away and the family being broken up. (See chapter 3.) The victim may also be placed in the invidious position of being told that a much-loved brother or sister will not be abused because of her continuing co-operation.

One of the most difficult aspects of sexual abuse and also one of the least acknowledged by the public is the ambivalence about the abuse and the guilt feelings many victims experience as a result of their own sexual arousal during the abuse, which can lead them to become trapped in abusive situations. The abused child often feels that she must have wanted the abuse in some way. She is afraid to tell as she fears that others will blame her as much as she blames herself. Abused children may even seek out the abuser when they need love and affection because their emotions have been manipulated by this trusted adult.

Adult and child victims of sexual abuse often need a lot of reassurance that although they experienced physiological arousal in their bodies while being abused, this does not remove any of the responsibility for the abuse from the abuser.[3] The victim needs to understand that her body can respond without her consent. Victims also need to come to terms with how their emotions have been manipulated by the abuser for his own sexual satisfaction. Understanding these and other complexities of the abuser/abused relationship is part of their difficult journey towards recovery.

One common reason given by victims for not telling of the abuse they experienced is their fear of what would happen to the abuser if they told.[4] This is particularly pronounced if the abuser is a family member. These fears are very real, especially in older victims who are aware of media reports of abusers being sent to prison. The victim may feel the need to 'sacrifice' herself to preserve the family unity, particularly if she already has an ambivalence about her own role in the sexual activity. I strongly believe that the availability of a community-based treatment programme for abusers, together with a greater emphasis on treatment rather than punishment, would encourage more victims to break their silence. (See chapter 10.)

Sadly, many children simply do not tell anyone that they are being abused because they have nobody to tell. This is a reflection of their isolation and possibly also indicative of the presence of other problems in their lives. Instead, they learn to survive within the abusive relationship by means of developing one or more of the following defensive behaviours.[5] The more extreme and severe the trauma of the abuse, the more profoundly the child will take on such strategies as a means of coping. The most significant defences used by such children include:

1   Denial: In this way, abused children convince themselves that the abuse is not happening.[6]

2   Disassociation: During the sexual abuse experience, children may actually have the sensation of leaving their bodies and 'floating' away from what is happening in order to escape the full impact of the trauma.

3   Splitting: This involves the child separating the good and bad aspects of herself and sometimes also of the abuser. For example, the child may develop two or more distinct selves, one being the good child and another being the bad child. The bad child is the one being abused because of her badness. This enables such children to understand why someone they love can hurt them while at the same time protecting that relationship.

4   Projection: By locating unacceptable feelings of helplessness, terror, rage and the desire for revenge elsewhere, the child manages to survive.

5   Identification with the abuser: By identifying with the abuser, the child makes the abuser part of herself, which makes the abuse bearable. Children who have been abused may act violently towards other children or show little sympathy for other children's distress.

6   Hypervigilance: In this case, the victim is always on edge in a vain attempt to prevent the abuse from happening. The child may become very sensitive to noises, smells, et cetera associated with the abuse.

7   Overly responsible behaviour: Here, the child believes that if she was a better child, the abuse would stop. She takes on adult responsibilities such as cooking, cleaning or looking after other children as a means to improving her behaviour.

8   Overly nurturant behaviour: Abused children who have not been nurtured recognise the need for love and caring. As a result, they are often very loving and caring towards other children and animals. Their secret desire is that someone will nurture them also.

9   Complete self-reliance: The awareness that adults cannot be trusted results in some children trying to do everything for themselves.

10   Self-nurturance: Abused children may find ways to soothe themselves through rocking, having a developed imagination, reading constantly or overeating.

11   Rigid thinking: In an effort to gain control over what is happening to them, some children engage in magical thinking or behaviour. For example, some children leave the light on in their bedroom in the belief that this will prevent the abuse (which usually occurs in the dark) from happening. Others say a particular combination or number of prayers believing that this may prevent the abuse.

12   Self-abuse: Abused children may inflict pain upon themselves (e.g. cutting or burning themselves) in order to have some control over their bodies. Physical pain is often more manageable than emotional pain.

The use of these coping strategies by children will depend on such things as the severity of the abuse, the relationship between the victim and the abuser, and the age and psychological maturity of the child when the abuse occurs. The presence of other problems such as alcoholism or violence in the home may prevent older children from admitting to themselves what is actually happening and therefore reduce the chances of them telling a significant adult about the abuse.

One of the most hopeful developments in the last decade is the huge growth in awareness of sexual abuse. This has enabled many adults – who were previously unable to report their abuse – to come forward. In one survey, adults in their thirties admitted that the main reason they now felt able to talk about their childhood sexual abuse was that they now felt safe.[7] This feeling of 'being safe' was due to a number of factors, one of which was how time and distance lessened the power of the abuser. For some, the sense of being safe came from the fact that they were now well into their adulthood. They had established their own identities and felt emotionally strong enough to confront the enormity of what had happened to them as children. For others, the fact that the abuser was now dead enabled them to speak out.

Overall, the greater public recognition of child sexual abuse now, as compared to when these victims were children, greatly influenced the decision of adults to talk about their abuse for the first time. David Finkelhor, one of the leading researchers into child abuse in the United States, believes that the changing social context can reduce the incidence of sexual abuse.[8] The adult victims who have come forward in the past fifteen years are people who experienced their sexual abuse and then grew up during a time of great ignorance and secrecy about abuse. Because of this, their sense of being different, their shame of carrying such a secret and their isolation contributed to their pain and suffering and the overall trauma of the abuse.

In the past ten years, sexual abuse has become a problem with a great deal of public visibility. More and more children are receiving information about sexual abuse through the introduction of Stay Safe-type programmes in schools as well as from their parents and the media. The present generation of abused children is much more likely to have heard of sexual abuse. Finkelhor believes that they are therefore much more likely to tell someone about their abuse, and much more likely to get their hands on information which will help them make sense of what has happened. They are also more likely to know of others who have been sexually abused.

That children be believed when they report sexual abuse has been found to be one of the best preventions of long-term trauma.[9] We hope that the change in society's attitudes towards sexual abuse will result in many more children being believed today than a generation ago.

A higher level of public awareness, reduced stigma and a greater general ability to intervene and help those who have been sexually abused are important steps towards reducing the trauma of those who suffered sexual abuse alone. Unfortunately, the prognosis is not so good for those individuals whose experience of sexual abuse is compounded by other serious personal and family problems.

2

Boys as victims of sexual abuse
Why boys are often believed to be less damaged than girls

When the reality of the sexual abuse of children was first brought to public awareness in Ireland in the mid-1980s, sexual abuse became synonymous with men sexually abusing little girls. Men were the enemy; girls and women the victims. This understanding arose as a direct result of the work of the Women's Movement, which courageously highlighted the prevalence of sexual abuse in an era when there was serious scepticism about its existence. Most of the information at that time was obtained from adult women who were coming forward to disclose that they had been sexually abused as children by men.[1] Other women responded by setting up voluntary support services for these women. These services were seen as being provided only for women by women, and in some centres men were completely excluded.

In this climate where men were viewed only as the aggressors and the enemy, few men were able to admit that they too had been sexually abused as children. Thus the myth became established that boys were much less likely than girls to be sexually abused. And while men continued to hide their experience of abuse, there were no parallel male support groups to match those provided for women, and there was no outcry about the damage being done by sexual abuse to young boys.

Even when information became available suggesting that many of the men who had sexually abused children had been sexually abused themselves, the protection and treatment of boys received little attention. Sexual abuse was viewed predominantly as a female problem.

Researchers now recognise that this misleading view of sexual abuse was reinforced by early statistics which confirmed that more women than men had been sexually abused as children.[2] The results of these early surveys are now viewed as being flawed as a result of men being asked the wrong questions. Men in general simply did not admit to being abused in childhood in response to open-ended questions (often asked by young male academics) as to whether they had been abused. Research findings have been shown to vary greatly depending on the ability of the interviewers to make the men feel at ease. The reality is that most men tend to reveal their sexual abuse only after months of counselling for other psychological, social and sexual problems.

The myth that boys are less likely to be sexually abused than girls is reflected in child protection programmes such as the Stay Safe programme currently being implemented in Irish primary schools. Most child protection programmes were adapted from the empowerment models used by female social workers in rape crisis centres with adult female clients. One expert shows how these programmes are failing to meet the needs of boys in the following ways.[3]

They fail to take into account the fact that boys

- live in a more highly sexualised peer group environment

than girls

- are handling their genitals on a daily basis and are not subject to the same notions of body privacy and genital secrecy that girls are
- are sexually curious at an early age, which allows paedophiles to tap into this curiosity by introducing pornography and conversations about masturbation and oral sex before they introduce sexual touching
- often find dirty talk exciting, especially if they lack relevant sex education and their parents are considered to be unapproachable
- sometimes view genital touching and oral sex as pleasurable and loving, especially in the early stages of the seduction process when they are the recipients of attention and no demands are made for reciprocation
- blame themselves for the abuse, especially if they liked the attention which accompanied it
- sometimes go looking for sexual contact when they associate it with affection and approval

These points highlight the lack of sexuality education for boys. While girls are also deprived of appropriate education and information about their sexuality, the fact that they have periods and can become pregnant means they are more likely than their male peers to get some information. Most men who have been sexually abused state that their lack of sex education contributed to their abuse.

Sex is used in advertisements to sell just about everything, and from a very young age children are exposed to sex on television. Yet children are not given the necessary information to make sense of the highly sexual environment they live in. Adults often conveniently deny that children are sexual beings and that boys have sexual urges and sexual interests from an early age. If not understood and accepted by adults, this immature or childish interest in sexuality can then be manipulated by an abuser. (See chapter 9.)

At most, the boy child may have some sort of understanding that sex is about men and women and making babies. The activity of the abuser often has no association with sex for him. Skilled abusers will make the boy feel special and feel that the sexual activity is an integral part of the special relationship. Few boys actively dislike the sexual activity when it is part of this attractive package of adult attention and affection. It also feeds into their natural curiosity about sex. All of this combines to leave the child feeling guilty and responsible when the realisation of the true nature of the relationship emerges.

Boys are particularly vulnerable to male abusers who act as father figures. Researchers highlight what I hear all too often from adult male victims: that is, that their own fathers failed to provide them with the physical affection, hugs and cuddles which they needed. One researcher went so far as to say that 'of all the factors which contribute to the vulnerability of boys to sexual abuse, the lack of a warm, affectionate, father figure appears to be the most significant of all'.[4]

There are two important reasons why men find it so hard to admit that they have been abused. Firstly, they often do not consider what happened to them to be sexual abuse.[5] The fact that they enjoyed some aspects of the sexual behaviour, or that they did not resist it, prevented them from seeing it as abuse. This is particularly so if the abuser was a woman, given that the dominant male culture tells boys that sexual experience with older women is the ultimate in sex education.

The second reason why many men do not admit to having been sexually abused (even if the experience was deeply disturbing and distressing) is their fear that if they tell someone, they will be seen to be weak or even homosexual.

Sex role stereotyping of men and women is such an integral part of our lives that we are seldom aware of how much we accept it unquestioningly.[6] Yet much of the difficulty which men have in admitting they have been abused is caused by such stereotyping. We are subtly informed through advertisements, films, books, music videos, children's toys and so on of conventions such as 'Boys don't cry'. They are still expected to grow up to become men who are strong, dominant, self-reliant, and successful. While the female stereotype may be changing faster than its male equivalent, girls are also still expected to grow into women who are emotional, nurturing, caring, soft and sympathetic.

Boys know from their earliest awareness the importance of fitting in and they discover very quickly that life can be hell if they appear 'different'. Being 'different' usually involves showing characteristics that are considered 'girlish' and consequently 'weak'. If a boy shows sensitive, vulnerable or emotional reactions, he risks being rejected, shunned, ridiculed or bullied. Little wonder that many boys find it easier to pretend to be what they are not. How much more difficult it is then for boys who have been sexually abused to cope with the gap between their experiences and feelings and those of how men and boys are supposed to be.

In the area of sexuality, men are often presented as the dominant, knowledgeable, confident sexual partner – what one man in therapy described as the 'John Wayne in *The Quiet Man*' syndrome. Women, by contrast, are often shown to be passive, weak, powerless and submissive. Neither stereotype is helpful. Sex role stereotyping permits society to feel sympathetic more easily to women who are victimised and consequently much less sympathetic to men who are victimised.

In Ireland, the case of Lavinia Kerwick, a young rape victim, personified the weak and vulnerable female. At the time of writing, six years after the crime was committed, she continues to have a high media profile as a female victim whose life has been destroyed by the abusive act of a man (albeit a seventeen-year-old adolescent). Even in the ultimate abusive crime of murder, female victims have – during the last few years in Ireland – received more sympathy and media attention than their male counterparts. The murder of a woman by a man is viewed as a more horrific crime than that of a man by another man, or indeed by a woman. A real man is supposed to be able to protect himself in every situation as his sex role model is that of protector and aggressor, not victim. It is also important to note that the portrayal of women as weak and helpless slows down their recovery from abuse and sometimes even perpetuates the damage.

Boys who have been sexually abused cannot be expected to be immune to all of these culturally defined stereotypes for boys and men. It is very difficult therefore for them to see themselves as victims. As men are not supposed to be victimised, boys who have been sexually abused often grow up to regard themselves as very inadequate men. They will tell no one for fear of being seen as weaklings. Many of the men whom I have met in my work have gone to great lengths to present themselves as macho men as a reaction to this fear. Another even more distressing fear for many of them is that they are homosexual. In Irish society, to be gay is still widely regarded as shameful and this further increases their anxiety.

Like their female counterparts, one of the most difficult aspects of the abuse for men is their recall of their sexual arousal as a result of the sexual activity.[7] For men, this raises one of two disturbing questions: 'Am I gay as a result of the abuse?' or 'Was I abused because I was gay as a child?' The male victims I meet often need a lot of reassurance about the capacity of the child's body to respond physiologically to physical stimulation, regardless of who is doing the stimulation. It is sometimes helpful to remind them that most small boys quickly discover that rubbing their penis produces different sensations to rubbing their nose and that these pleasurable sensations are an integral part of childhood. (See chapter 9.)

As adults, male victims (like female victims) tend to forget the age difference between themselves and their abusers. Focusing on this helps them understand that the sexual intent was solely on the part of the adult abusing them and that their involuntary response to the abuse was normal. As with girls, the sexual abuse of boys usually takes place within the context of a trusting relationship. It is this pairing of sexual activity with affection and attention which is so devastating. Boys who have been sexually abused by men or older boys are very confused about their own sexuality as a result. Simply liking another man can add to their fears of being homosexual.[8]

Some men I have met have joined the gay community as a way of ending their confusion about their sexuality. These young men will often feel they are gay as a result of being abused. The young gay community in Ireland appears to provide a very supportive framework for these men, who often feel a sense of alienation as well as having low self-esteem as a result of the betrayal of trust they experienced.

Other male victims have an inability to feel sexually desirable at all. The shame that they feel in relation to abuse connects shame with sexuality in a way that can lead to a number of sexual dysfunctions such as the inability to achieve or maintain an erection, premature ejaculation, compulsive masturbation or the inability to separate sex from humiliation, shame and pain.

Another fear felt by men who have been sexually abused is that they will become abusers. This fear arises out of the much-publicised fact that many men who sexually abuse have themselves been abused in childhood.[9] While this is true, what is much less publicised is the fact that the majority of sex abuse victims do not go on to become abusers – a case of the glass being regarded as half-empty rather than half-full.

The limited research which has been done in the area of symptoms suffered by male and female victims of sexual abuse indicates that boys suffer from the same symptoms as girls.[10] Both may experience fears, sleep difficulties and distractability. However, there is one significant difference in the female response to abuse. Girls tend to respond to the trauma of being sexually abused with what are called 'internalising behaviours' (e.g. becoming withdrawn and anxious, developing headaches and stomach-aches, regressing by thumb-sucking or bed-wetting, developing eating disorders, abusing drugs, mutilating their bodies). Boys, in contrast, have been found to respond to the trauma of the sexual abuse with 'externalised behaviours' such as acting aggressively, killing or torturing animals, acting in a sexualised manner. This latter behaviour helps us to understand why more male victims than female victims go on to be abusers themselves.

One researcher suggests that the sexually abused boy faces a choice.[11] If he accepts the messages he is getting from society about how men are supposed to behave, then he will respond by denying to himself the pain he feels. He will not talk about it and will probably make extra efforts to conform to the acceptable male standards as a result of his fear of appearing in some way different because of his abuse.

This particular study suggests that the men who fail to come to terms with the conflict they feel regarding male sex roles are the ones most likely to become abusers. Their denial of their own feelings also makes it difficult for them to empathise with victims. The confusion between power and abuse contributes to the possibility of this repeating tragedy. The boy will have had the experience of powerful adults abusing that power. This is most damaging if the person abusing him is also his main role model. In this case, the male victim is likely to draw the conclusion that to be a man, he must be abusive. Identifying with the aggressor therefore gives the victim a sense of control and power which he desperately needs. The only way he can empower himself seems to be by turning someone else into a victim.

In my work with male sex offenders, I have observed how important it is for many of them to be seen as hard, macho men whose lives centre on sport and the pub. Having a woman in what they see as an authority position, as a therapist in their group treatment, can be very challenging for them. This, in itself, has resulted in useful exploration of how threatened they feel in this reversal of their expectations.

Some male victims of sexual abuse deal with the conflict in another way by questioning and redefining male sex role expectations.[12] Their personal sense of being different pushes these boys to find ways to do so. Through this process, they can also allow themselves to experience the pain and sometimes even to seek help. Coming to terms with the fact that their abuse had made them different from their role expectations also meant that they were much less likely to go on to be sexual abusers themselves.

However, there is yet another group of men who have learned to cope in a less healthy way by becoming powerless and remaining in the victim role throughout their adult lives.[13] These boys see no other options in life than the roles of abuser and victim. Knowing what it feels like to be a victim, they are determined never to abuse another person. The role of victim is so familiar to them that they can carry it easily into all of their interactions with others. This results in their expecting to be, and often being, taken advantage of.

Alternatively, the boy who has been sexually abused may respond not by becoming an abuser or a permanent victim but by becoming a protector.[14] This is a response to his understandable fear that children are in constant danger from adults. He may be attempting to give other children the protection he needed but did not get himself. He may also see his role as protector as the only way to achieve non-abusive closeness to other people. Men often meet this nurturing protective need in a positive way by working in the helping professions.

The acceptance of the vulnerability of boys in relation to sexual abuse is a necessary first step in its prevention. It is hoped that the increasing number of boys reporting current sexual abuse at the hands of the clergy and other trusted caretakers will give others the courage to disclose their own abuse. We have to question how we, as a society, continue to make it difficult for boys to come forward with our failure to challenge the stereotypes of acceptable male behaviour.

I am, however, encouraged by the increasing number of adult men (not abusers) who are disclosing sexual abuse. I am particularly heartened by the tiny trickle of men coming forward as a result of their anxiety that they are at risk of sexually abusing children because of their difficulties in dealing with their own abuse. In this there lies true hope that support and help for these victims at this stage will prevent them from crossing the taboo boundary and becoming the next generation of abusers. As a direct result of this work, we can hope that we are enabling at least some children to have a childhood free from the trauma of sexual abuse.

3

What happens to the victim once the abuse is publicly revealed

Victims of sexual abuse are usually thought of by the public as helpless, passive individuals who must be rescued from their situation. Both they and their abusers are often viewed as having had no existence prior to the abuse. Consequently, once they are rescued from the abusive relationship, all is deemed to be well. Problem solved, end of story.

This snapshot view of the lives of those who have been sexually abused is, of course, oversimplistic. Yet, in the incompleteness of the picture which the public get from media reporting of such cases, it remains the dominant image we have of victims of abuse. Only unusual cases and trials are newsworthy and these tend to concentrate on the most extreme cases.

In this chapter, I look at the consequences for the victim in the immediate aftermath of her abuse being publicly revealed. How children cope with what happens after they have disclosed the abuse depends on their age, the developmental effects of the abuse, the nature of the relationship with the abuser, and the family supports. What happens is obviously very different for young children who have no control over the official interventions which must follow once their abuse is made public. Older victims have more choices about the course of action taken.

How and why younger children tell depends very much on the age of the child, the nature of the abuse, and the quality of the relationships the child has with other adults and children. One study of eleven-year-olds who had disclosed their abuse showed that 29 per cent told their mothers and 27 per cent told a friend.[1] Twenty-two per cent of the children said that they had told someone about the abuse because they knew it was wrong, 18 per cent because they did not want the abuse to continue, 16 per cent because they were angry with the abuser and 14 per cent because they had found someone they could trust.

When sexual abuse occurs within a family (and incest broadly includes sexual activities initiated by any adult who plays the role of a family member in the life of a child), the characteristics of the family are important.[2] This is not just because we know that sexual abuse is more likely to occur in certain families but because the level of support that the child receives from the family when she discloses the abuse is critical. Tragically, if there is a history of sexual abuse going back several generations in the family of the abused child, the child may have very damaged parents who are unable to respond appropriately. (See 'The Family Therapy Approach to Understanding Sexual Abuse' in chapter 6.) The child victim may then have to cope not only with the impact of the sexual abuse itself, but with what is called the stigmatisation as a result of telling (i.e. the abuser may blame and denigrate the victim, others in the family may also put pressure on the child to 'keep a secret' and there may be a lot of hostility towards the child in both the family and the community, particularly if the abuser is popular and well thought of).[3] Child victims may also pick up on attitudes of shame from others about the sexual activities which they have been forced into, and most insidiously, the victim may also get the sense of being 'damaged goods' as a result of the abuse.

The immediate psychological effect of such responses is for the child victim to feel guilt, shame, lowered self-esteem and a sense of difference from others. Long-term, this damage can result in a sense of isolation, drug/alcohol abuse, self-harm, criminal involvement or suicide.

Therefore the sexual abuse itself and the family dynamic the victim is part of are the most significant sources of trauma. What happens afterwards is, however, often a source of secondary trauma for the child. Front-line child protection professionals have an extremely difficult role to play in balancing the protection of the child with a belief that 'it should not hurt to help the child'. The belief that a child is being sexually abused may therefore give rise to two distinct types of legal cases: criminal proceedings which involve the prosecution of the alleged abuser, and/or civil proceedings which may determine such matters as whether it is safe for the child to remain within the family.

Guidelines have been drawn up to ensure that there is as much liaison as possible between health professionals and the police in order to reduce the trauma for the child.[4] The child may still have to be interviewed, and one of the main problems identified for victims has been the number of interviews they are subjected to. Children who feel guilty and ashamed about what has happened must repeatedly recount the stories of abuse, often to strangers, in the interests of justice. This connects them further to painful memories and reinforces their feelings of guilt and shame.[5] Young children may also require medical examinations. All of the evidence needed to validate that the child has been abused may have to be gathered under great time pressure to prevent the child from being intimidated into withdrawing what they have said.

When the abuse has happened within the family, the child is not always believed and supported by the mother and has to be taken into care. For some victims, their experiences are so horrific and there is such a complete lack of anything good or nurturing within their families that their removal to a place of care and protection is experienced as a relief. For most children, though, in spite of the sexual abuse trauma, their family is still all they know and being removed from it may be experienced as a punishment for telling.

In one study in which almost half (40 per cent) of the children who had been taken into care reported that they were glad to be safe from the abuser and from verbal attacks from their mothers, 70 per cent of those children still said that being away from their families was the most difficult thing they had to cope with.[6] When the abuse occurs within the family, professionals need to acknowledge that the relationship between the child victim and the abuser is often very complex. While some abusers do threaten the child to ensure that she does not tell, it is more common for the abuser to enmesh the victim into a relationship which the child experiences as good. When the sexual abuse is just one part of a relationship in which the child also gets a lot of attention and affection from the abuser, the upheaval that she experiences when she tells can leave her feeling guilty and confused. This is also true for other victims whose disclosures of abuse sometimes happen only after the abuse has ended.

Adult victims who are courageous enough to lift the lid off the secret of their abuse may experience many different responses from their families. Often caught up in their own problems, the last thing the family members want is for the victim to involve professionals in the dynamic of abuse. In one poignant case reported in the media, a woman of twenty-seven was disowned by her mother for disclosing the horrific physical abuse to which her father had subjected her for many years. The judge described the young woman as 'lonely, isolated and deserted by her mother, the one person who she thought would stand by her'. This remark reflects the myth of the family as always caring and supportive, which those of us working in the area know to be untrue.

The victim being unsupported by the family and community unfortunately happens more than the public may wish to acknowledge. The older victim may also be caught between pressure from professionals to report the abuse in order to protect other potential victims and pressure from the family to withdraw the allegations as the price to be paid for remaining within the family.

In one case, in which a number of sisters in one family were abused by their father, the breaking of the years of silence by one of the young women resulted in huge upheaval within the family. Only one sister supported her in her allegations. Two others denied their own experience of abuse and were extremely angry with the sisters who were insisting that the truth be told. The mother refused point-blank to hear what her daughters had to say (one presumes she already knew) and colluded with her husband in his denial. The sons in the house also sided with their father, and the two sisters found themselves isolated and rejected by both immediate and extended family members, who labelled them as 'troublemakers'.

Other older victims are sometimes pressurised into making a statement to the police by overzealous professionals before they have an opportunity to work through their anger, grief and guilt about what happened. The desire to punish the abuser on the part of the professional can take precedence over the needs of the victim.

I know of one young woman whose father sexually abused her once within the context of what she considered to be an otherwise good relationship. She had reacted promptly by re-porting to a professional what he had done. The professional re-sponded by putting strong pressure on her to make a statement to the police. This she reluctantly did. All she wanted was that her father should receive help to make sure that he did not do to anyone else what he had done to her. The fact that her statement to the police resulted in her father receiving a prison sentence left her feeling betrayed by the professional and bitterly regretting her actions.

Professionals need to explain to all victims in a more honest and open manner what might result from them reporting their sexual abuse.[7] The making of a statement to the police about all of the details of the abuse can be extremely stressful and embarrassing.[8] Once the victim has made her statement, she has no control over what happens. She may have a very long wait before the Director of Public Prosecutions makes a decision as to whether the case will go to court or not.

In the trial of an alleged sexual abuser, the victim is often the vital prosecution witness. The purpose of the proceedings is to establish the guilt or innocence of the accused. The trial takes place in open court and the standard of proof is 'beyond reasonable doubt'. This is very different from what happens in a civil case which decides what arrangements should be made to benefit the child and in which the best interests of the child are paramount.

In criminal cases, the victim's evidence is usually the key evidence of the prosecution case. This is because physical evidence of sexual abuse is seldom available, and since secrecy is essential to enable the abuse to occur, there is seldom any form of corroborative evidence. The victim therefore is only a witness and the outcome of the case depends on whether the court believes the alleged abuser or the child. Consequently, the victim is at risk of being confused and bullied by skilful defence barristers in order to create an element of reasonable doubt and secure an acquittal for the alleged abuser.

Research shows that many children have found the experience of giving evidence and being cross-examined in a criminal trial in the presence of their alleged abuser to be extremely intimidating and upsetting.[9] It is acknowledged that some children would be damaged by giving evidence against the alleged abuser and that they should not have to do so. If their testimony is crucial to the prosecution, this may mean that the case against the alleged abuser is withdrawn. This highlights the difficulty of deciding how to balance the best interests of the individual child against the wider need of society for protection against child sexual abusers. New technological methods have been introduced to try to overcome these difficulties. These include allowing the admission of videotaped interview evidence from child witnesses and the use of a live television link to allow the child to be cross-examined in another room in court. Screens may also be used to protect the child from seeing the alleged abuser if they are cross-examined in court. These measures came into force in England and Wales in 1992, following the report of the Pigot Commit-tee. In Scotland it has been possible since September 1991 to use live TV links for the evidence of children in any trial, not just sex abuse cases.

The Child Care Act 1991 in the Republic of Ireland has also made laudable provisions to ensure that the child's interests are represented in civil cases. The Act empowers a court to make a child party to all or part of care proceedings and, where appro-priate, to appoint a solicitor to represent the child. In addition, children who are too young to communicate their needs effec-tively to a solicitor can now have a 'guardian *ad litem*' appointed by the court. This involves a professional (not involved in the case), who is skilled in communicating with young people, speaking to the court on the child's behalf.

The nature of the relationship with the abuser also influences the impact of the trial on adult victims. If the abuser is not a family member and he had abused a number of victims, the en-suing court case can be used by the victims to express their anger and to exact retribution. This was evident in a high-profile case in Ireland in 1998 involving a swimming coach (Derry O'Rourke) who had numerous victims. Now adults, they in-sisted on detailing in court what he had done to them sexually even though his guilty plea had made this unnecessary. For these victims, this further punishment through shaming their abuser appeared to be therapeutic. This can be compared to the contrast-ing experience of a young woman I know who was abused by a close family member. Her abuser also pleaded guilty, but in spite of this, all the intimate details of the sexual activities were not just read aloud in court but published in the local paper. In a small community where, as the victim put it, 'even the dogs on the street' knew her identity and that of her abuser, the trauma of this was described by her as being much worse than the trauma of the sexual abuse itself.

No two cases are therefore alike but the 'social pornographer' role of the media in publishing the details of the victims' trauma does need to be queried.[10]

While it may be convenient for the public to see abuse as a triangle consisting of abuser, victim and rescuer, the reality is not so simple. It must be stressed that the person who is responsible for the damage done to the victims of abuse is first and foremost the abuser. Abusers and victims do not, however, exist in isolation. The impact of sexual abuse also needs to be viewed in terms of the entire impact of the abuse on the victim's family and community.

That the victim of sexual abuse really be listened to remains the challenge for those who have the interests of the child at heart.[11] The child's voice is very easily drowned out by the louder and more authoritative voices of those who focus only on protecting the child sexually and punishing the abuser.[12] The victim's rights to have her voice heard in decisions affecting the future must be acknowledged. Legislation to empower children is crucial and invaluable. Implementing that legislation requires a commitment to ensuring that the voice of the child being heard represents the complexities of each individual situation.

4

Sexual abusers
Mostly male but female abusers do exist

One of the main messages the public consistently gets from the media is that sexual abuse is perpetrated by men. The idea of a woman being an abuser is, in the words of one female abuser, 'the greatest taboo of all'.[1] This belief that women do not abuse is so strong that in a 1996 survey of over two thousand children in Britain and Ireland,[2] no women – not even mothers, sisters or grandmothers – were included in the list of potential abusers while all possible males – fathers, grandfathers, uncles, step-fathers, stepbrothers, brothers-in-law – were listed.

One researcher reports that men and boys are responsible for 95 per cent of child sexual abuse.[3] There is, however, increasing evidence that abuse by women has often been overlooked. Research in Australia has indicated that women perpetrated between 14 and 27 per cent of the abuse of boys there, and up to

10 per cent of the abuse of girls.[4]

In the past, the sexually abusive female was described as very emotionally disturbed, psychotic or sociopathic. However, more recently, this definition has been found to be limited. Female abusers, like male abusers, fall into many different categories, from those who have been abused themselves to mothers who sexually abuse their children.[5]

The victims of female abusers suffer from this lack of awareness of their existence. We must remember that the physical abuse of children was only acknowledged in the 1960s and the emotional abuse of children only in the 1970s. It was not until the 1980s that the existence of the sexual abuse of children was widely recognised. It would appear therefore that the acceptance of women as abusers will become the issue of the next decade.

When the Women's Movement pioneered the recognition of the widespread abuse of female children by men, this gave many women the courage to report their childhood experiences of abuse. However, as discussed in chapter 2, this perception of abuse as being a female problem initially prevented male victims from coming forward. The limited perceptions of who abusers are are now also having repercussions on victims of female abusers. One researcher noted that the very reluctance of women to accept that women offend means that their female victims 'have felt doubly silenced'.[6]

Women also find it difficult to accept the existence of the sexual abuse of boys by women. When a male 'survivor' phone-in in Western Australia showed that more than a third of the callers reported sexual abuse by females, the women organisers of the phone-in rejected the information and sought an alternative explanation: that the calls were hoaxes perpetrated by paedophiles to implicate women and diminish the seriousness of their own offences.

Gender values and expectations are other reasons why the public at large fails to recognise the damage done to boys by female abusers. Like it or not, there is still widespread acceptance, if not promotion, of the idea that sex with older women is the ultimate educational experience, a belief typified by the film *The Graduate*.[7]

Female sexual abusers fall into four broad categories: those who are coerced into abusing children by men; those who sexually abuse their own children, often when they are very young and over a long period of time; those who abuse adolescents; and those who were themselves abused as children and then go on to repeat the abuse.[8]

Female sexual abusers who act under the control of men are the group that the public can most identify with. They include, in the most extreme cases, reviled women such as Rosemary West and Myra Hindley. Many of the women in this category claim that they were forced by men, often their partner, to participate in the sexual abuse of children.[9] In one study, all of the women in this category had been sexually abused as children by at least one male.[10] The male co-offender also usually physically, psychologically and sexually abuses his female accomplices.

The second category of female abuser is the mother who abuses her children. Some women sexually abuse their teenage sons under the guise of love and affection. This type of abuse has received very little recognition simply because there has been a lack of awareness of its existence. Over the past number of years, I have come to question such matters as the family sleeping arrangements and bathing habits in families where teenage boys are referred for disruptive behaviour in school and the use of sexual language. The following is a checklist of questions therapists should ask mothers of such children to identify whether sexual abuse is occurring:[11]

1 Was there sexual or physical abuse and/or neglect in former generations of the family?
2 Are there problems relating to alcohol or drug abuse in other family members?
3 What is the quality of the relationship between parents like?
4 Is the mother socially isolated?
5 Is the mother currently abusing drugs or alcohol?
6 How is affection physically expressed in the family?

7　What is the mother's involvement in bedroom, bathroom and bathing habits in the family?

8　What are the family sleeping arrangements?

9　What are the parents' history of sexual experiences?

10　How was sexuality expressed in the parents' families of origin?

11　Is the child confused or uncomfortable with the mother's expression of affection?

From the above questions, four major factors have been identified as increasing the likelihood of a child being sexually abused by his/her mother.[12] These are as follows:

1　the child's father being absent – either completely physically absent due to death or separation, or seldom at home because of work or alcohol abuse

2　the child's mother being socially isolated with few or no friends and feeling very lonely

3　the child's mother having a history of abusing alcohol or drugs (prescribed or illegal)

4　the mother having a history of sexual abuse

The following case clearly illustrates the complexity of mother–son sexual abuse.

Twelve-year-old Eoin was referred to me because of his aggressive, disruptive behaviour at school. His teachers were also concerned about his sexually explicit language and his drawings of sexually explicit female pictures in school. Eoin was the only child of Marian and Thomas. Both in their mid-forties, they were a middle-class couple with a good income. Thomas, however, was an alcoholic and spent all of his time after work in the pub. Marian was the only child of a very demanding and dependent mother. She did not work outside the home and had become depressed and addicted to prescribed medication. She felt that her life had passed her by and her only interest in life was her son.

Marian had no sexual relationship with her husband and they slept in separate rooms. In therapy, it emerged that Marian asked Eoin each night if he wanted to sleep in her bed and if he said no, she withdrew her affection and was cold and distant with him. When Eoin did sleep in her bed, Marian admitted that she tickled him all over his body. She claimed, however, that there was nothing sexual about this as Eoin was too young to get an erection. Marian was very reluctant to discontinue these sleeping arrangements, saying that 'you might think it is wrong but we call it loving'.

Another mother moved during the night from the bed she shared with her husband into her ten-year-old son's bed. The reason she gave for this was her dislike of sleeping with her husband when he came home after drinking. There were other empty beds in the house but she chose to sleep in the single bed with her son, claiming that he enjoyed all the cuddles she gave him. She was unable to make any connection between her son's numerous psychosomatic illnesses and her behaviour.

In other cases, the blurring of boundaries between what is legitimate care of the child and what is sexually abusive involves mothers who insist on bathing and sharing a bath with their older sons, and mothers who regularly apply cream to the genital areas of pre-teen children to prevent soreness. American studies have identified mothers who use enemas on children in a forceful, aggressive and intrusive manner which violates the children's personal boundaries.[13]

The mother–son incest type of female abuse is frequently the most difficult for boys to reveal. They are often enmeshed in a confusing emotional relationship with their mothers, and this type of abuse is further complicated by the cultural myth that mothers are asexual and that males are always sexually dominant and aggressive. All these factors lead the boy to interpret the abuse as a form of affection, particularly if force and violence are not used. Boys abused by their mothers often assume responsibility for the abuse. Researchers also point to the following reasons why boys rarely report sexual abuse by their mothers:[14]

1   boys cannot become pregnant
2   mothers are viewed as 'all-good'

3 boys are too ashamed to reveal sexual activity between themselves and their mothers
4 society's myth that boys are not affected by being molested by
   women
5 the lack of knowledge – on the part of both professionals and
   male abuse victims – that there can be a connection between
   mother–son incest and the difficulties which male victims of
   sexual abuse experience as adults in interpersonal relationships

Mother–daughter incest is also difficult for victims to reveal.
The greater tolerance of physical intimacy between mothers and
daughters makes it more difficult for victims to acknowledge
when these contacts become incestuous. Research points to sexual contact varying from voyeurism to kissing and fondling to
mutual masturbation.[15] A useful guideline for professionals
when defining mother–daughter incest is: 'Would the behaviour
described be considered as incestuous and sexually abusive if the
father were the initiator?' The victims of mother–daughter incest
were found to have a number of serious problems including depression, migraine headaches, psychotic behaviour, homosexual
acting out and bed-wetting.

Another more passive but damaging form of abuse by
mothers is when they have an active involvement in father–
daughter incest cases. Some mothers – particularly if they have
been sexually abused themselves – give silent consent to such
abuse by remaining passive about an incest situation.[16] They
may also be frightened of the abuser's violence and fearful of the
family being broken up.

A mother who has few resources of her own may be unable to
protect her child and thus collude with the abuse. Such women
use the psychological defensive techniques of denial, repression
and minimisation in order to avoid confronting the incestuous
situation. They will insist that because there was no intercourse,
no harm was done. Alternatively, they will actively endorse the
abuser's excuse that he was only teaching his daughter the facts of
life.

Other mothers feel sexually rejected by their husbands and

view the abused child as an enviable younger rival. Ways in which the mother deals with these feelings include either blaming or disbelieving the abused child, which also allows her to deny her own guilt about having failed to protect the child.

One researcher, Estela V. Weldon, distinguishes between male and female sexual perversion in the following way. While both men and women use their reproductive functions and organs in sexually abusive acts, men tend to focus on their penis while women use their whole body since their sexual organs are more widely spread.[17] Weldon goes on to explain that this may be the basis on which male abusers in general externalise their response to sexual abuse while women tend to internalise theirs. (See chapter 2.) Perhaps more controversially, Weldon also concludes that when women direct their sexual perversions internally, this can involve damage to their own bodies (e.g. self-injurious behaviours, eating disorders and so on) and damage to their children – who were, if you follow the argument, born from them. Such women (i.e. mothers who abuse their children) may even decide to have a baby to force their partner to commit himself to the relationship and to treat her with some respect as the mother of his child. These women may then go on to treat their babies as dehumanised objects whose role is to be used or abused according to the mother's needs. According to research, they start to abuse their children within the first two years of their lives.

The abused infant protects herself against the abuse by withdrawing from the mother and making herself unable to think as there is so much real pain. She is unable to develop any sense of trust or to establish intimate relationships. And so the abuse cycle continues into the next generation.

Early emotional deprivation is recognised as a feature in the lives of women who treat children in a sexually abusive or perverse way. Such things as a history of neglect, abandonment, humiliation of gender, physical abuse or sexual abuse are factors which tend to perpetuate abuse from one generation to the next. Mothers who have been badly damaged by their own abuse are unable to separate their children's needs from their own. Those who have been victimised by their own mothers then go on to victimise their own children, often treating them as objects who are there only to satisfy their whims and bizarre expectations. Women who abuse adolescent males may tend to talk about it as if they were realising a toyboy fantasy. Such women may perceive the sexual relationship as a love relationship but it is very much about having power over the adolescent. The most high-profile example of this category of female abuser is the thirty-four-year-old American schoolteacher Mary Kay Le Tourneau, whose seduction of her thirteen-year-old male pupil resulted in him fathering two of her children.

Another category of female abuser is those women who have been sexually abused themselves. Like some male abusers who have themselves been abused, they repeat the pattern of abuse. While girls in general tend to internalise their responses to abuse (by developing self-mutilation behaviours, eating disorders, depression and so on), there is a certain percentage who will project their experience of abuse onto others.[18] The following case study shows how one teenager recognised this tendency within herself.

Noreen, a twelve-year-old girl, was referred for counselling after revealing that her fifteen-year-old female cousin had sexually abused her. The abuse had occurred on a number of occasions when the girls were sharing a room. Noreen's cousin had inserted her finger into Noreen's vagina and had masturbated herself by lying on top of Noreen. Noreen had found the abuse both physically painful and frightening. Her cousin had threatened to kill her if she told anyone what she had done to her. Noreen, a bright, articulate and very angry child, was concerned when she recognised her own urge to repeat the abuse. She described how she found herself looking at younger children and thinking of ways of getting them on their own in order to do to them what her cousin had done to her. 'I know it's not right,' she said, 'but it's not fair. She hurt me and I want to make someone else hurt the way I did.'

The final category of female abuser is the older, unrelated female, for example babysitters and women who physically

confine or use threats of violence to force a male child to participate in sexually abusive acts.

There is a widespread belief among the general public that
abuse by women is less damaging and therefore less important
than abuse by men. This belief reflects the perception of the penis
as a dangerous weapon. The female, who is biologically without
one, is then deemed to be less harmful.

Women who sexually abuse their children have been found to
suffer more from their abusive actions than male abusers.[19] They
are also often more aware of the deep psychological wounds and
long-term consequences they produce. This can lead them to ask
for professional help, which, unfortunately, is not easily available. It is, however, believed that the recovery rate for this type
of female abuser is quite high.

Female abusers, regardless of which category they fall into, remain the perpetrators we try to forget. Society continues to
ignore their existence and the psychological and sexual damage
they cause. Victims of sexual abuse by women have been found
to feel more damaged by the psychological aspects of the abuse
than by the sex.[20]

While some of the cases we now encounter in everyday clinical practice involve damaging and invasive inappropriate sexual
contact between mothers and their sons, female abusers are, unfortunately, also emerging as being as capable of sadistic and perverted forms of sexual abuse, accompanied by physical and
emotional abuse, as their male counterparts.

Adult female offenders are, in general, very subtle in their
abuse. Detection by outside agencies is rare, except in cases where
the mother is alleged to have aided and abetted the father's sexual
abuse. Reports suggest that mother–son incest cases are likely to
be revealed only in long-term therapeutic settings.[21] If the abuse
of the boy is non-violent and involves a women, then it is often
not considered to be abuse.[22]

Some offenders, including women, videotape their abuse for
circulation to paedophile rings. It is these tapes that have provided proof of the unthinkable and will, at last, make it easier

for children who allege that they have been sexually abused by women to be believed.

The sexual seduction of the young adolescent boy by the older, unrelated woman is, however, one form of abuse by females about which society remains ambivalent.[23] There is far less ambivalence when the victim is a young girl and the abuser an older man. Proof of this dual attitude can be found in a comparison between media coverage of Mary Kay Le Tourneau's affair with her pupil and the recent failure of the new cinematic version of Nabokov's *Lolita* to find a distributor in the USA. In Le Tourneau's court case, the defence lawyer claimed that she had found the man of her dreams but he was thirteen.[24] The reality is that for the older woman abuser, like her male counterpart, such relationships are about control and power rather than love.

In Ireland, the number of cases involving female sex offenders is low, and to date, no custodial sentences have been imposed. In one case, a twenty-four-year-old woman was charged for her sexual relationship with a fourteen-year-old boy. However, her sentence was suspended so that she could receive treatment for alcohol and drug abuse. In court, the woman was described as 'not having a full understanding of morality' and as having been 'in love with the boy'.[25] While such an outcome is welcomed by those of us who advocate treatment as a necessary response to such cases, it is not acceptable to use alcohol, drug addiction or, indeed, love as an excuse for sexually abusive behaviour. It is also frustrating that many of the immature young male counterparts of this woman would not be shown such leniency. They are instead given custodial sentences, regardless of the fact that they are unlikely to receive any treatment in prison. (See chapter 10.)

The first steps towards accepting the existence of 'the greatest taboo of all' must involve each individual challenging his/her own resistance to the reality of women as potential sex abusers. Only then, as has been shown historically within other domains of abuse, will victims of female abusers feel able to come forward and seek help to recover from the abuse they suffered.

5

Why all abusers are not the same

As the group of men file into the treatment room in Letterkenny, what is immediately obvious is their 'normality'. They would blend in easily anywhere as men of different ages and backgrounds congregating by chance – at a football match, in a pub or in a church. They range in age from those in their early twenties to those in their late fifties. Some are well dressed and at ease in their clothes; others have made an effort to look smart but still look uncomfortable in their 'good' clothes.

Some will chat easily together in the waiting room. Others will remain aloof, nervous and edgy about what is ahead of them, or will want to feel that somehow they are different from the others. They may like to believe that their sex offending was different – that it was less serious than that of the others. Maybe they had abused only once, or they had abused only because they were drunk.

Whatever their thoughts or the nature and degree of their abusive behaviour, what these men have in common is that they all have sexually abused children. They would not be attending for treatment if they had not been 'found out', which usually happened when their victim got the courage to tell. This is a fact that they constantly need to be reminded of, especially when they protest that they will never be at risk of offending again.

While statistically, these offenders can be placed into factual categories, according to their age, marital status, age of victim and so on, the reality is that, like all men who sexually abuse children, they are indistinguishable from 'the man in the street'. I believe that it cannot be repeated often enough that the vast majority of children who are abused are not abused by paedophiles or sex-starved monsters, but by immediate family members, whether male or female. (See chapter 4.) In the vast majority of cases (85 to 92 per cent), those who abuse are relatives or family friends who are known and trusted.[1] This fact still appears to have escaped the general public, who, in spite of the acres of newsprint on the topic of abuse, retain dangerous stereotypical images of sex offenders.

The many and varied public perceptions of child sexual abusers outlined in 1979 still hold true today:

> The child offender [is imagined] to be a stranger, an old man, insane or retarded, alcohol or drug addicted, sexually frustrated and impotent, or sexually jaded and looking for new 'kicks'. He is 'gay', and recruiting little boys into homosexuality, or he is 'straight', and responding to the advances of a 'sexually provocative' little girl.
>
> ... He is sometimes regarded as a brutal sex fiend, or as a shy, passive, sexually inexperienced person. He is oversexed or he is undersexed ... the product of a sexually permissive and immoral society with lax attitudes and laws regarding sexuality that stimulate and encourage him through the availability of pornography, drugs, alcohol, and sex outside marriage.
>
> Some see such behaviour as reflective of lower-class

mentality and morality, poverty and the lack of education. Others attribute it to a criminal personality. And still others, when the offender is an adolescent, take the position that this behaviour is typical for a sexually maturing male, nothing more than experimentation.[2]

While there are case examples which support each of these images of the abuser, they are the exception rather than the rule. It is unfortunate that these exceptions receive the most publicity, and perpetuate the notion of a 'them and us' scenario in relation to sex abusers for the public. (See chapter 7.)

These popular stereotypes also make the child abuser as unlike the ordinary person as possible. The main television presentation of sex abusers as sinister, shadowy silhouettes with distorted voices reinforces the tendency to demonise them as a group. These images are easier to accept and understand, and allow many of us to hold onto the illusion that the world is a safe place. They also assist us in our denial of our own capacity to engage in abusive behaviour.

So how can we begin to understand this demonised and reviled group? We have first to look at the terms used to describe sex abusers as this is where much of the confusion arises. The widespread use of the term 'paedophile' (applied to all individuals who sexually abuse children) in the media is very inaccurate and misleading. At particular times during the past few years, depending on the latest revelations of abuse, 'paedophile' became synonymous with 'priest', 'west of Ireland farmer' or 'Belgian child murderer'. Thus, the leering, sinister face of Fr Brendan Smyth in Ireland, the unspeakable evil perpetrated by Marc Dutroux and his associates in Belgium and the sadistic brutality of the men in the Kilkenny case and the McColgan case, merge in the public mind to create a composite picture of the dreaded bogeyman of our worst childhood nightmares.

The application of the term paedophile to all sex abusers has also been found lacking by feminists.[3] They fear that the term distracts from the abuse of power which is central to all sexual exploitation of children. This distraction then allows the abuser

to hide behind a label which suggests an abnormality over which
he has no control rather than focusing on his personal responsibility for the abusive actions.

Who then are the abusers who can accurately be described as
'paedophiles'? Ray Wyre's definition of paedophiles as 'those
men who have a primary sexual preference for, and sexual arousal to, children' best clarifies the term.[4] The paedophile is also described as being 'fixated' in his sexual preference for children.
(Ironically, with its current association with child sex abuse, the
term 'paedophile' comes from the word 'paedophilia', which lit-
erally means 'love of children'.)

As a means towards understanding better the motivations of
these abusers (and therefore knowing how best they can or cannot be treated), professional careworkers have further subdivided
the category of fixated paedophile into three groups: 'moral conflict paedophiles', 'social conflict paedophiles' and 'sociopathic
paedophiles'.[5]

There are, however, many other sex offenders who do not
have a primary sexual preference for, and sexual arousal to, children. These non-fixated offenders can be categorised into two
separate subgroups: transitional offenders, and regressed or compensatory offenders.

Transitional Offenders are men who experience normal sexual
arousal with adult women. However, due to a lack of social skills
and other deficits discussed elsewhere, they have never had any
normal sexual experiences with their own age group. They then
turn to children to meet their sexual needs. Regressed or compensatory offenders are often married men or men who have
adult sexual partners. However, they compensate for difficulties
in their adult relationships – either real or imagined – or their inability to come to terms with life-stage challenges, by using children (often their own) to meet their sexual needs.

In addition to the two main categories of fixated paedophile
and non-fixated offender, there is growing concern about a third
category of offender. These are juvenile offenders – adolescents
and children who abuse other children. This group has received

little media attention and there is a lack of public awareness of the numbers of juvenile offenders.

Sexually abusive behaviour by adolescents and children has historically not been considered as serious a problem as sexually abusive behaviour in adults.[6] This is due to a mistaken belief that the young person will 'grow out of it'. Unfortunately, the opposite is the case and there is now evidence that without treatment, such young people continue their sexual abuse into adulthood. It is a daunting fact that international research into this area indicates that between 34 and 56 per cent of all cases of child sexual abuse are perpetrated by adolescents.[7] One study indicated that 36 per cent of all reported cases of child sex abuse in the Republic of Ireland were carried out by adolescent offenders.[8] Many adult offenders begin their sexual abuse of children in adolescence. In one study, 50 per cent of adult sex abusers reported that their deviant sexual arousal began before they reached the age of eighteen.[9] Treatment of adolescent offenders needs therefore to be given priority, particularly as treatment programmes for adolescents have been shown to have good success rates in preventing reoffending.

In the following pages, I will give a description of each type of sex abuser, along with case histories. Through this analysis, I hope the reader will begin to understand how sex abusers are sometimes as far from their stereotypical media portrayals as you or I.

The 'moral conflict paedophile' is the first type of fixated paedophile. This sex offender has a compulsive sexual preference for children. He is aware, however, of the wrongness of his sexually abusive activities with children. He usually has a history of emotional or psychiatric disturbances that stem from a conflict between his sexual need for children and his guilt about that need.

He is frequently a good organiser, may be involved with youth groups and is genuinely interested in children in a non-sexual way. His compulsion to abuse is, in some cases, related to his own abuse in childhood, and he may, in fact, find himself re-creating the same situation in which his own abuse occurred. He may also believe that, since he is in control, the activity will not be as demeaning, violent or harmful to the victim as his own abuse was. Afterwards he may feel guilty and ashamed, and may consider reporting his crime to the police. He may view masturbation as a safe substitute for abuse without realising that it will only serve to reinforce the desire to repeat the fantasised acts.

An example of this type of abuser is the young man who abducted and sexually abused a child in a case which was widely reported in the Irish media in the summer of 1996. This man then gave himself up to the authorities because of his fear that he would be unable to prevent himself from repeating his actions.

The use of medication to reduce the sex drive (and in so doing reduce the internal feelings of conflict) is sometimes useful in treatment with this group of paedophiles. A controversial law passed in California in 1996 forces repeat child abusers to undergo 'chemical castration' through the administration of weekly injections of a testosterone-inhibiting drug to reduce their sex drive. This is an example of the misguided generalisation of a form of treatment which may be beneficial with one specific type of child abuser but is certainly not appropriate for all abusers.

The following case history illustrates some of the features of this type of offender.

Patrick, a respectable, mild-mannered, pleasant man in his fifties, presented himself for treatment when his sexual abuse of young boys over a thirty-year period was eventually discovered. Patrick was unusual in terms of the men who attend the treatment programme in that he had not engaged in any sexually abusive behaviour during the previous ten years.

His sexual abuse of children followed a pattern in that he abused one child a number of times and then did not abuse for a number of years. He had a total of seven victims over the thirty years. It was only when one of his victims, now an adult, revealed what had happened that a case was taken against Patrick.

The community he lived in was devastated by the sexual abuse revelations as Patrick had devoted all his spare time to the development of facilities for young people and had been instrumental in getting many of them involved in sporting activities. His interest in children's welfare was genuine and even his harshest critics could not deny the positive contributions he had made to the lives of so many of them. However, the boys he abused were devastated by both their experience of sexual abuse and the abuse of the trust they had had in Patrick. He had singled them out for special attention and individual coaching and then sexually abused them. Their confusion and their fear that they would not be believed had prevented them from telling anyone what had really happened during this 'special' time with him which the other children envied.

In treatment, it emerged that Patrick had struggled all of his life to control his compulsive sexual preference for children. He had even married and was a good and caring husband but he was never sexually aroused by his wife. After each episode of abuse, he was tortured by feelings of guilt and anxiety that he would be found out. He plunged himself into his work in his attempt to block out what he had done. Not surprisingly, he was regarded as a workaholic, as this helped him to control his sexual feelings. He showed a great deal of will-power in extending the time between his cycles of abuse, up to the ten years before he was found out.

In spite of the public outrage and anger against him, it was almost a relief for Patrick that his shameful secret was, at last, out in the open. He was genuinely remorseful and was, in treatment, able to take on board the reality of the effects his abuse had on his victims. This he had blocked out for many years, using the fact that they had never told on him as a way of minimising to himself the harm he had done to them. Patrick was also able to develop more realistic strategies to ensure that he would not re-offend, including, of course, having no further contact with children. His wife and some of his close friends remained supportive towards him and he is now attempting to rebuild his life, while continuing to attend relapse prevention aftercare. His victims are the people most damaged by Patrick's sexually abusive behaviour and their needs take priority. However, the other innocent victims of his abusive behaviour – his wife and family, whose lives have been shattered – are also deserving of sympathy and support.

The 'social conflict paedophile' is the second type of fixated paedophile. This offender sees nothing wrong with sexual activity with children, and argues that it is society's attitude which is wrong. Unlike the moral conflict paedophile, these abusers have no feelings of guilt about their sexual preferences. They see themselves as being lovers of children, and believe that their sexual activity with children is part of a loving relationship.

An extensive interview with a paedophile on an Irish radio station (RTÉ Radio 1) in 1994 (which caused widespread outrage at the time) portrayed to the public this type of abuser. He articulated very well the type of 'twisted thinking' known as cognitive distortion used by these men to justify their activities. He rationalised his behaviour by the fact that none of the boys abused had 'said no' to the sexual activity, and that he had never used force. He genuinely believed that the sexual activity was mutual and part of a loving, caring relationship. In common with other social conflict paedophiles, he saw the law as being out of touch with reality, and felt that he was doing no wrong. He was not challenged with the question of why, if his relationships with the boys were based on love and caring for them, those relationships ended when the boys became too old for him.

These paedophiles see themselves as part of a sexual subculture, and, like any subculture, they seek reinforcement of their views (in their case that sexual activity with children is not wrong) by linking up with other paedophiles. The publication in an Irish Sunday newspaper in August 1996 of the sordid transcript of a telephone conversation between two paedophiles exposed the public in a particularly graphic way to the grim reality of the nature of their activities.

Social conflict paedophiles also use the Internet, and join clubs

such as NAMBLA (North American Man–Boy Lovers Association). This provides them with a focus for their sexual perversions and enables them to share information on their victims
and sexual experiences. They also publish pro-paedophile litera-
ture and lobby for changes in the law to lower or remove the age
of consent for sex. The increasingly exposed, murky world of sex
tourism has grown around catering for the sexual preferences of
these men.

They are generally thought to be unlikely to benefit from
treatment as their understanding of the nature of relationships is
so distorted and damaged. Only legal sanctions, such as the prosecution in their home countries of those who go on 'sex tourism' trips, is believed to force them to modify their behaviour.
However, more Irish-based research is needed in this area as abusers of this type who are identified at an early stage may be influenced at least to the extent that their twisted thinking is
challenged.

The 'sociopathic paedophile' is the third type of fixated paedophile. This offender differs from the last two categories in that
he does not identify at all with the victim, who is seen only as an
object, and used as a means of sexual gratification. This type of
abuser has no capacity to have any form of relationship with the
victim, and does not need to use the twisted thinking of the other
categories to justify his activities. These abusers take advantage of
any sexual opportunity that allows them to control a victim.
They sometimes use criminal methods such as abduction and
murder to avoid detection. Many of them do have age-appropriate sexual preferences while some have an exclusive preference
for sex with children. Such people lack a conscience and have
no regrets about their behaviour. They are frequently violent,
punitive, and have no moral constraints about what they do.

The sociopathic paedophile may be a father whose authority
must not be queried, or a totally unscrupulous adult who has no
regard for, or understanding of, the feelings of others, and who
may lie, cheat and manipulate without compunction in his
dealings with others. Research on psychopaths shows that these

abusers are incapable of 'learning from their mistakes' and experience no guilt feelings, and hence are not deterred by punishment or prison sentences. It is questionable whether the layperson's popular solution of castration would have any effect on this type of offender as the sexual activity is such a secondary part of their activity.

It is this type of paedophile who inspires most horror, and who gains most publicity. They include the Marc Dutroux's of this world, and, as they are essentially amoral, they are not amenable to treatment. Our encounters with such offenders have indicated that they are not suitable for group treatment, as is illustrated by the following case study.

Fred attended the treatment group for six weeks as part of his assessment. He had systematically sexually and physically abused his daughters over a number of years. He showed no remorse for what he had done, and had no capacity to understand the effects of his abuse on his victims. He was totally self-absorbed, and turned every conversation around to himself and how badly treated he had been by his family. The very fact that his abuse had been reported, and that as a result of this he had been excluded from the family home, was seen by Fred as him 'being got at' by everyone.

He was very arrogant, and felt that he was superior to the other men in the group. He saw himself as being omnipotent, and became very angry when confronted about his abuse by team or group members. Fred believed that his family belonged to him. He provided for them, and he had the right to do what he wanted to them. He tried to use the same domineering, bullying bluster in the group that he had used to intimidate his family. His word was not to be questioned by anyone. The only person he considered to have been abused was himself as a result of his family's lack of gratitude to him. It was felt that, if he had been allowed to remain in the group, it would have been only a matter of time before he exploded emotionally, and physically attacked either a team or group member.

While the activities of the last two categories of paedophiles in particular obtain most publicity and media headlines, the majority of children are not abused by fixated paedophiles. They are abused by men whose sexual preference is adult, but who at different times in their lives, and for different reasons, look to children to satisfy their needs. These 'non-fixated' offenders are described by professionals as 'transitional', and 'regressed' or 'compensatory' offenders, in contrast to the 'fixated paedophile' whose sexual preference is for children.

Scanning the inside pages of any daily newspaper reveals, in small tucked-away columns, the frequency of abuse (so frequent that it no longer merits headlines). Fathers, grandfathers, uncles, brothers, family friends and neighbours stand accused with depressing regularity of the sexual abuse of the children in their lives.

The first of the two types of non-fixated offenders is the transitional offender. These men usually do have the capacity to become sexually aroused by their own age group, but they lack the social skills to form age-appropriate relationships. Instead, they turn to children to meet their sexual needs, and their offences against children are usually their only sexual experience. The recall of their sexual activity with a child is used as a fantasy to masturbate to, and this in turn reinforces their paedophile sexual preference.

A typical profile of those we have met in our treatment programme is that of a shy, mild-mannered male in his late twenties who is interested in females of the same age but either lacks the opportunity to socialise or feels inadequate both in relation to his male friends when at discos and so on, or, more particularly, when alone with a woman to whom he feels attracted. He is often aware of his 'shyness', and hence each encounter with a woman is of huge importance, and each 'failure' is perceived as a rejection which confirms his own view of himself as being unattractive, useless and powerless to find a girlfriend.

Because of his shyness, he is often more at ease with children, and is often accepted by them as a trusted friend. Hence, he may often be asked to do the babysitting or childminding by other family members. Combined with sexual fantasies, this may lead to an abusive act which, if the child does not tell, can progress to more serious abuse which can then be repeated on a regular basis.

The limited ability to control his impulsive behaviour is another factor in such cases, due to the abuser's emotional immaturity. This problem may be further aggravated by alcohol abuse to help him interact socially or to dull his feelings of rejection.

This type of offender is regarded as being treatable. In addition to undergoing all of the elements of a treatment programme outlined in the appendix, these men benefit from social skills training programmes where they gain an ability to form friendships with their peers. They also benefit from a specific behavioural treatment programme of orgasmic reconditioning which involves replacing the dangerous fantasy involving sexual activity with a child with an age-appropriate sexual fantasy.

The following case history is a sad yet hopeful example of this type of sex abuser.

Andrew was referred for assessment following the disclosure by his nine-year-old niece that he had been sexually abusing her for two years. The abuse had occurred on a regular basis, coinciding with Andrew's overnight stays in his sister's house when he slept in his niece's room. The abuse had initially involved fondling of the child's genital area, and had progressed to Andrew rubbing his penis against the child's vagina and ejaculating.

Andrew was in his early twenties and one of a large family from a remote rural area. He lived at home with his parents, helping them to run the small family farm. His brothers and sisters were married and had families of their own. Andrew's only social outlet involved visiting other family members. He did not drink, and although he attended football matches, he did not socialise afterwards.

He used to go to dances when he was younger, but he never had a girlfriend. He felt at ease only with his family, and in particular with his nieces and nephews. He always brought sweets for them, and they loved to see him coming. They sat on his knee, and he tickled them and got involved in all their games. The niece whom he abused was especially fond of him, and she liked the idea of him sleeping in the spare bed in her bedroom.

Andrew recalled how on one occasion, several months before the more obvious abuse began, he had become sexually aroused when his niece was bouncing around on his lap playing a 'horsy' game. He was surprised by this, but enjoyed the sensation. After that, he sought out this niece for rough-and-tumble games, deliberately bringing her into contact with his penis, and thus causing an erection. He then masturbated in private. Anyone observing him playing with his niece at this stage would not have been aware of what was happening.

The early abuse was successfully cloaked as play, and Andrew convinced himself that there was nothing wrong with what he was doing. After all, he was just playing with his niece and she was enjoying the fun with him. Over time, he began to masturbate when he had no contact with her, using the recall of his sexual arousal when playing with her as his sexual fantasy.

The first overt incident of abuse with his niece occurred when she was asleep, and he pulled down her bed quilt and fondled her genitals. This was repeated on a number of occasions, and each time Andrew convinced himself that he was not harming her as she was asleep.

As the severity of the abuse increased and it was no longer possible for him to hold on to his belief that she was asleep, he used the fact that she did not respond or ask him to stop to enable himself to believe that he was not harming her. He experienced intense guilt and anxiety after each abusive incident, but as the day progressed, and it became obvious that his niece had not told, his anxiety and guilt subsided. In the weeks between the incidents of abuse, he continued to masturbate, using the recall of his sexual activity with his niece as the source of arousal.

When his niece eventually told her mother that Uncle Andrew was doing 'dirty things' to her and that she did not want him to sleep in her room any more, Andrew's world fell apart. His family members were devastated and angry. The police were notified, and Andrew admitted what he had done and made a full statement. However, his niece's family decided that they would not pursue the matter legally, and, in the absence of her making a statement, no charges were brought against him. Counselling was arranged for the young girl, and Andrew was banned from having contact with any of his nephews or nieces. In addition, his family insisted that Andrew should attend a treatment programme for sexual abusers.

When he first came for assessment, he was painfully shy and lacked social skills. He avoided all eye contact, and his speech was slow and hesitant. He slumped in the chair and twisted his hands together continuously. Treatment was a long and slow process. Andrew was actively suicidal as a result of the disclosure of his abuse of his niece. He considered suicide his only way of avoiding the pain he was experiencing, and on several occasions drove down to the sea with the intention of drowning himself.

Careful counselling with him on the effects that his suicide would have on his family, and on his niece in particular, acted as a deterrent. Andrew was adamant that he still loved his niece. The fact was stressed to him that his suicide would be a further abuse of her, as she would then feel responsible for having told her mother what was happening. In addition to the shame of his family knowing what he had done, Andrew found it difficult to cope with the loss of contact with all of his nieces and nephews, whom he loved. They had been the only people in his life who made him feel good about himself.

Slowly, and falteringly, Andrew outlined in group therapy sessions the details of his cycle of abuse and took responsibility for it. The treatment group became his focus for living, however painful the experience of being confronted with what he had done. After one year of treatment, he was referred to a social skills group in addition to attending the sex offenders' treatment programme. He benefited immensely from this, and the contrast in his appearance was dramatic. He looked more confident and he was able to speak clearly with great openness and honesty.

It was only at this stage that Andrew disclosed details of his own abuse. It emerged that he had been systematically abused from the age of seven by an older male cousin when the cousin stayed overnight with the family. Ironically, the abuse mirrored his own abuse of his niece. His cousin had shared his bed as well as his room, and Andrew's response to the abuse was to pretend to be asleep. He had not protested even when the abuse had progressed to painful anal rape. His cousin had threatened to kill him if he told anyone about the abuse. The large, affectionless family described by Andrew, where high levels of violence were the norm, was hardly conducive to a young boy revealing something that he had no name for, or no language to describe.

Andrew remained in the treatment programme for two years. He continues to attend relapse prevention after-care days. His family have discussed his progress with treatment team members, and he is now allowed contact with nieces and nephews again, although he is still not welcome in the home of the girl whom he abused. He is not allowed to be alone with children, or to engage in body-contact play. He is, however, slowly establishing other social contact outlets, going to pubs with other single men after football matches, and then to dances with them. He is more at ease about asking women to dance, and, while he has not yet established a relationship with an adult female, he is moving in that direction. He now uses sexual fantasies involving adult females when masturbating.

I believe that as long as he continues to do this, and to progress in establishing age-appropriate relationships, he is unlikely to reoffend.

A distinction must be made between those sex offenders whose abuse of children is the result of a deviant sexual preference for children, and those whose abuse of children is situationally induced or opportunistic and occurs within the context of a normal adult sexual preference.

It is these so-called regressed or non-fixated offenders who need to be the focus of more attention as this is the group which the public has most difficulty in identifying as being a danger to children. The fact that they are responsible for such a high percentage of the abuse of children also highlights the need for child protection programmes to emphasise the possible dangers associated with 'nice', 'familiar' men rather than 'stranger danger' types.[10] (See the case of Gerry and the Doherty family in chapter 6 for an example of the regressed offender.)

Juvenile offenders are a mixed group of boys and girls who are not as easily categorised as adult offenders. Mostly boys, their first sexual offence will have been reported before they reached the age of eighteen. Very young children are also capable of sexually abusing other children. In one American study, children between the ages of six and twelve were identified as the perpetrators of 13 to 18 per cent of all child sexual abuse.[11] Nearly all of these children had themselves been sexually abused.

Research has focused on what characteristics are particularly prevalent among adolescents who are sexually abusive. There is general consensus that the development of sexual deviance in young people is due in large part to experiences the child has in his early family life combined with temperamental factors which predispose him to behaving impulsively.[12] The more severe his own experience of abuse was (physical, emotional or sexual), the more severe his abuse of others is likely to be.

Another worrying factor is the connection made by researchers between exposure to sexually explicit materials at an early age and subsequent sexual abuse of younger children by adolescents.[13] In one Irish study, physical abuse, parental separation and school-related educational and behavioural difficulties were more common in the lives of sexually abusive adolescents than in a control group of non-abusing adolescents.[14] Other researchers found that physical abuse by one's father, combined with sexual abuse by a male and low levels of attachment between the mother and child, contributed to the development of sexual aggression in adolescent males.[15]

Such evidence makes the abusive behaviour of Bobby in the following case study more understandable.

Bobby's eleven-year-old sister, Sarah, told her best friend at school that Bobby hurt her and did dirty things to her. It emerged that Bobby had attempted to have sexual intercourse with his sister on a number of occasions. Sarah and Bobby's parents were separated and his father abused alcohol and then physically abused his wife and both his children. Bobby's mother worked part-time and she too was a heavy drinker. The family had had previous contact with the social services because of reports that the two children were left on their own in the house. Bobby had also been diagnosed several years earlier with specific learning disabilities. He did not get very good results at school even though he was an intelligent boy. His frustration and embarrassment at his poor performance resulted in him opting out and spending little time with his own age group. Instead, he spent a lot of time with his unmarried uncle, who was also a heavy drinker. Bobby eventually revealed that he had been sexually abused by his uncle. His sexual abuse of his sister could be viewed within the context of his 'externalisation' of his own distress, i.e. he responded in an aggressive way against her rather than becoming depressed or self-destructive.[16] His abusive family environment had left him with an inability to form intimate relationships or to feel empathy with others.

When we meet such young offenders, the implications for prevention are very clear. It creates a challenge for individuals and communities. Children like Bobby cannot be expected to thrive in such adverse conditions. Children must first be protected from deviant developmental experiences. Then those who do suffer, like Bobby, must be allocated adequate resources to enable others to help them learn how to behave appropriately. Only then will the risks of such children continuing their abusive behaviour into adulthood be minimised.

6

The complexities of
sexual abuse
The psychological perspectives

There is general agreement that we can place the men who sexually abuse children into one of two main categories, i.e. the fixated paedophile and the non-fixated offender.[1] The former are men who experience sexual arousal only in relation to children while the latter are men who do not experience deviant arousal in relation to children but who act out sexually with a child as a way of dealing with their inability to form or maintain intimate relationships with adults. That the ordinariness of either group of men is their major distinguishing characteristic still does not answer the question of why they abuse.

No amount of categorisation helps in the understanding of why 'normal' adults break one of society's oldest taboos, and sexually violate the most vulnerable members of our community. Even more incomprehensible to the layperson is why some of those children who have been sexually abused grow up to become abusing adults. Why would one want to inflict on others what was experienced as so painful for oneself at an earlier stage? In this chapter, I will outline some of the psychological theories which help in answering the disturbing question of why adults sexually abuse children.

THE PSYCHOANALYTIC APPROACH TO SEXUAL ABUSE

In some psychoanalytic theory, the origins of paedophilia are believed to lie in childhood experiences. Freud believed that paedophilia was a form of neurosis.[2] He saw it as a regression to infantile sexuality or a regression to the phallic stage of development due to unresolved Oedipal conflicts. He also believed that one of the paedophile's greatest unconscious fears was that of being castrated. As a child, the paedophile wanted to be sexual with his mother but feared castration from his father if he acted on his desires. As a result of this fear, the paedophile is unable to deal with normal adult heterosexuality. He therefore resorts to safer forms of sexual expression with children.

Other psychoanalysts see the nature of the parent–child relationship as contributing to the development of paedophilia.[3] One theory applicable to homosexual paedophiles regards the paedophile's attraction to children as a form of self-recognition. This is believed to result from a child having no father present either emotionally or in person and a mother who is also not available to him. With no parental model to identify with, he is thus unable to resolve the Oedipal conflict, which depends upon the boy identifying with his father in response to the threatened loss of possession of his mother. In this void, the child substitutes himself as the love object. He grows up into an adult who narcissistically remains in love with the child he was. This is impossible, so he must project his love onto other children of a similar age to his love child. These children then become love objects for him.

Another theory is that paedophilia may develop as a result of a narcissistic relationship between the child and the mother.[4] Here, the mother loves herself excessively and regards the child as an extension of herself. The child thus acquires a narcissistic attitude, and as an adult, this is projected onto an idealised version of children. These paedophiles are thought to be attracted to children who remind them of themselves at a particular age.

It is true that many paedophiles are fascinated by and attracted to the qualities of children. Such qualities may not be physical or sexual but of a more general nature. In Britain, revelations about the homosexual composer Benjamin Britten and his friend Peter Pears regularly taking boys on holiday with them without sexually assaulting them sparked off a debate about whether there may be men who are attracted to children and enjoy their company but successfully control their sexual feelings.

THE SOCIAL LEARNING THEORY OF SEXUAL ABUSE

Another school of thought is that of Social Learning.[5] Here, it is believed that men who sexually abuse children have become conditioned to responding sexually to young, sexually underdeveloped bodies. According to this theory, these men learn over time to associate sexual arousal with encounters with children. This is believed to happen in the absence of normal adult sexual relations.

Although it is now recognised that not all men who sexually abuse children are sexually aroused only by children, Social Learning theorists point to what is known as 'classical conditioning' as an important mechanism in the process. The theory claims that young, pre-teen children are capable of sexual arousal and orgasm but they do not interpret the experience sexually until they reach their teens. Social difficulties with more mature partners later on (as experienced by many paedophiles) then rekindle this earlier sexual arousal.

One of the difficulties posed by the theory that sexual arousal by children is conditioned by the experience of sexual activity among young people of the same age is that the actual experience may be just one-off, or too occasional to establish conditioning.

This is where the very important role of sexual fantasies, which has implications for treatment, is recognised.[6] It is suggested that the memory of the first actual sexual experience becomes the basis of fantasies used in subsequent masturbation. The fantasy of sexual activity with a child becomes increasingly arousing through repeated masturbatory experiences. The original experience may also become distorted in recall, so that certain specific cues in the original experience grow in importance. In this way, an individual may become fixated on a particular type of child as a source of sexual arousal, and features such as age, hair colour or dress can become very significant, as in the following case history.

Richard, an unmarried man in his thirties, attended for treatment as a result of his sexual abuse of a young girl over a period of two years. The abuse had involved him putting his hand up the child's clothes and fondling her genital area, over her pants. He had also exposed his penis to her. He claimed that he had no wish to view the victim's genitals or to engage in any other sexual activity with her. He revealed during treatment that his sexual fantasies always involved a girl wearing pants. During one session, he revealed an episode when, at the age of thirteen, he was in a hay-barn with a girl of the same age. They engaged in sexual talk of the 'I'll show you mine if you show me yours' variety, then started climbing up onto the bales of hay in order to further their 'game'. The girl was in front of Richard, and he retains a very vivid image of his view of her white pants. At that moment the girl's father arrived, caught Richard by the scruff of the neck, and lectured him about 'spoiling the hay'. This was Richard's first and only sexual experience. His sexual activity was confined to masturbation, aided by an image of white pants. It can be speculated that the incident he reported became conditioned not just because of its sexual content but because of the added 'buzz' of the fear of being caught. A factor of his abuse of the child was his doing it in places where the risk of being seen was high.

It is a feasible theory that sexual arousal as a result of normal childhood sexual exploration becomes the basis of masturbatory fantasies for those individuals who, for various reasons, are unable to move on to normal adult sexual relationships.

PROBLEMS IN THE DEVELOPMENT OF ATTACHMENT BONDS AND INTIMACY

There is a much-documented link between childhood abuse and subsequent sexual offending. Figures vary as to the extent to which victims become offenders and repeat the abusive behaviour which they experienced as children. One researcher suggests that one out of every fourteen victims of abuse becomes an abuser.[7] Fifteen per cent of the men who have attended our community-based treatment programme have told us that they were sexually abused in childhood. However, our experience has been that, while many of the men initially stated that they had not been sexually abused, information which they later disclosed indicated that they had been subjected to sexually abusive behaviour which they regarded as normal.

Similarly, when asked initially about their early experiences, they glossed over the nature of relationships within their families, and described their childhood as being 'happy'. In the course of treatment, these same men disclosed enough to enable us to say that 99 per cent of the men we have worked with experienced both emotional and physical abuse as children. Common features were large, emotionless families, the presence of brutal fathers (many of whom were alcoholics) and inadequate mothers who were unable to protect them, but whom many of the men idealised.

We are constantly reminded of the wisdom of Alice Miller's words: 'No one who has had a healthy upbringing, that is, one where he/she had the experience of being validated as a person, and their vital needs of love, respect and understanding met, will feel the need to hurt or harm another individual.'[8]

While abhorring the abuse which the men we work with have perpetrated on children, it would be a hard-hearted person who would not be affected also by the grimness of their own childhood experiences.

After a number of years of running the programme, we became concerned about the difficulty we were experiencing in achieving our aims in the area of victim awareness. It is recognised that the capacity to feel empathy is one of the best safeguards against reoffending. Men who successfully gained insight into their offence cycle and the uses of defence mechanisms seemed unable to grasp how much their abuse damaged their victims. They appeared to have little understanding of what childhood was supposed to be about, and how sexual abuse would impact upon a child's emotional growth. Our sense was that even when the men were able to give the 'correct' responses, these were coming from the head and not from the heart.

We decided to focus more on the men's own experience of childhood, in the belief that only by getting them to relive their childhood emotional experiences could we get them to step into the shoes of their victims more effectively and empathise with them.

The stories which we heard greatly increased our awareness of the difficulties of achieving victim awareness in individuals who have never been able to reconnect with the frightened, confused children they once were. For example, we heard of the child whose father took a great interest in his homework. If anything was not to his father's liking, he was ordered to redo it with his father standing over him. The more flustered and unable to do the work the child became, the angrier the father became. He repeatedly hit him, shook him, and physically threw him across the room, all the time telling him how stupid he was, and how he would never be good for anything. The father of another child liked to keep him in suspense. He would point his finger at the child as he left to go to the pub and tell him that he would be 'in for it later'. 'It' involved savage, unprovoked beating which left the child believing that he must be very bad to need so much punishment.

We heard about another child who fled in terror with his

mother from his brutal father. He grew up into a man who considered himself a coward and inadequate because of his inability to protect his mother from his father's blows. Then there was the child whose mother believed that no other children were good enough for him to play with. Only she could take care of him, and she insisted on bathing him until he was a teenager. He in turn had to take care of her when she retreated from his father into his bed at night.

The litany of physical and emotional abuse recalled by the men was harrowing. Even more disturbing was their acceptance of their abuse as being the norm. In the absence of any positive nurturing experiences of childhood, these men had huge difficulty appreciating the damage they in turn had done to children by abusing them. Even those who reported having been sexually abused themselves as children had difficulty in relating their own pain and suffering to that of their victims.

In order then to try to understand the seemingly incomprehensible, how adults are able to sexually abuse children, we need to look at the effects of loss, abuse and psychological trauma on the attachment relationships of both children and adults.

What emerges most clearly from research on attachment is that the individual can exist only in relation to 'the other'. This finding is crucial to our understanding of human abusive behaviour. We now realise just how much human beings depend on their attachment to one another for their psychological wellbeing, and in particular how much children need to be securely attached to their primary caregivers, usually their parents.

It was the British psychoanalyst John Bowlby who made us aware of the crucial reciprocal relationship which appears to exist between the need for the 'other' and abusive behaviour.[9] A complex process of psychobiological attunement between the child and his caregiver is replayed throughout the individual's subsequent relationships and is at the heart of his attachment to others. This means that any disruption of this essential developmental process leads to serious long-term effects at both a psychological and a physiological level.

If the parent is neglectful, inconsistent, rejecting or abusive, the child will come to believe that he is unlovable and he will not acquire self-confidence, empathy or the skills necessary for the forming of affectionate bonds with others. We all have intimacy needs and research indicates that failure to meet these needs can lead to the sort of aggressive self-serving behaviour evident in adults who sexually abuse children.[10] It is suggested therefore that as a result of poor childhood attachments with their parents, sex offenders grow up ill-equipped to meet the demands of social and sexual relationships.

One researcher has extended this understanding of the effects of parent–child attachment to how it affects adult romantic relationships.[11] Children who are securely attached become adults who feel self-confident – they have a positive view of others and have all the skills necessary to establish intimate and fulfilling relationships.

However, an 'anxious-ambivalent' style of attachment is evident in adults whose parents were inconsistent, neglectful or rejecting. These adults desire intimacy but they are anxious and fear rejection. They think positively about others but lack any sense of their own worth. They are eager to get close to a partner but as soon as intimacy begins to develop, they become afraid and retreat. The most damaged children become adults with what is called an 'avoidant' style of attachment. This style results from having parents who were physically, sexually or emotionally punitive or rejecting.[12]

Avoidant types are divided into 'avoidant-fearful' and 'avoidant-dismissive'. Avoidant-fearful people have negative views of themselves and others, and as a result are afraid to form close ties for fear the other person will recognise their flaws and reject them. Any relationships they form are superficial and lack depth. Avoidant-dismissive people think well of themselves but see others as self-interested and uncaring and are therefore hostile towards them. Any relationships they form are fleeting and formed only to meet their own needs, such as sex, food, shelter or companionship.

Other researchers predict an association between each of these attachment styles and specific forms of sexual offending.[13] 'Anxious-ambivalent' offenders are likely to form an affectionate relationship with their victims. These are the offenders who describe their relationship with their victim as loving, and may claim to be 'in love' with them.

Aidan was one such offender who attended our treatment programme. He told the group of his devastation when, as a teenager, he was unable to maintain an erection the first time he tried to have sex with a girlfriend. His humiliation was compounded by the girl laughing at him and broadcasting to his friends his inability to perform. His next attempt to have sexual intercourse was with a prostitute, several years later. He felt that this would be a safer situation, but again he was unable to 'perform'. He then became worried that he was homosexual, and he retreated completely from the challenge of adult sexual relationships. In his later sexual abuse of a young girl he described how he liked to imagine that she was his 'proper' girlfriend.

His abuse of the child occurred in the context of a close affectionate relationship. Aidan distorted the wrongness of his abuse by projecting adult qualities onto the child. She became the loving, accepting partner he had never had. He reported that this fantasy was so strong for him that he never even considered the possibility of the child telling anyone about what he was doing to her. He did not believe that she would ever do anything that would cause trouble for him.

In another extreme form of this distorted view, one offender, aged forty-five, actually married the sixteen-year-old girl he had started to abuse when she was thirteen.

'Avoidant-fearful' offenders, on the other hand, are seen to seek out impersonal contact. These are the men who might molest children only once but have several victims. 'Avoidant-dismissive' offenders would also seek out impersonal contacts, but their hostility makes them more dangerous. They may be aggressive and sometimes sadistically brutal towards their victims and can be placed in the sociopathic category described in chapter 5.

All of this evidence that some sex offenders have significant problems with intimacy and experience severe emotional loneliness points to the need to address attachment deficits in treatment programmes. It is only through understanding these deficits that we can come to terms with the men's inability to respond appropriately to the distress of the children they abused. It takes a lot of supportive and challenging work in treatment before offenders are able to admit to the fact that they were aware their victims did not like what they were doing. The strength of their defence mechanisms and twisted thinking enables them to repress aspects of their abuse which they do not want to remember. The dismantling of the defensive mechanisms and the realisation of the full impact of their abuse on the child, whom they often claim to love, is a critical point in the treatment of the individual behaviour. The men's allowing into their awareness the frightened, confused, tearful or frozen-in-shock faces of their victims frequently results in traumatic re-experiencing of their own childhood abuse.

All of the strongly maintained defences which enabled them not just to abuse once, but to carry on abusing, crumble. It is at this stage that these men may become suicidal and feel overwhelmed by guilt and grief. It is also, however, the stage of treatment, if properly managed, which most significantly reduces the risks of reoffending. It is only when they become conscious of their own emotions that they are able to recognise and identify with the feelings of others. In order to enable them to become emotionally and personally responsible, therapists need to create a non-judgemental and trusting environment in the treatment setting in which there is no abuse of power and authority.

PROBLEMS IN THE DEVELOPMENT OF SELF-IMAGE AND SOCIAL SKILLS.

Research with sex offenders indicates that in some areas of functioning, they feel confident but in other areas, much less so. In this, they are similar to other non-offending individuals. However, there is evidence that the capacity of the offender to benefit from treatment is impeded by low self-esteem. This is true also in other problem areas such as addictions. Assisting all addicts to improve their self-confidence has been shown to increase the effectiveness of treatment programmes.[14] Increasing the self-esteem of the offender is therefore an important aspect of treatment, provided it is combined with changing his distorted thinking in other areas.

Social skills theories look at how underdeveloped social skills contribute to the choice of sexually abusive behaviour, particularly when the abuse involves a child of the opposite sex. Research has shown that sex offenders are less socially competent than non-offenders. Stress has also been identified as a factor which makes offenders look to children to satisfy their emotional needs.

One researcher in Australia, who assessed over eight hundred sex offenders, found that the majority of non-fixated offenders perceive themselves as powerless.[15] They see themselves as failing in their male role, and failing in that they are unable to develop and maintain relationships with women. These same men also have very traditional views about the roles of men and women. It is their inability to live up to gender role stereotypes which results in their feelings of self-doubt and overdependence.

These findings mirror our own experience with many of the men who attend our programme. Their relationships usually involve dependence, either passive or overly dominant, in which the man tries to control his internal insecurities by controlling the others upon whom he depends for emotional support. These men tend to sexualise their emotions and to discriminate good from bad relationships by the nature and frequency of sexual activity. They are very emotionally dependent on their partners, and any change in their partner's behaviour is viewed as a threat to which they overreact. They tend to adopt a victim attitude towards life, and feel 'hard done by'. They resort to using children as substitutes for adult partners because they see them as less 'powerful' than themselves.

Their offences therefore are usually brought on by some form of real or imagined threat to their dependence. The victim is usually a female child onto whom they transfer their dependency needs. The child is used as a non-threatening substitute to replace an adult partner. Unlike the fixated paedophiles, therefore, who have no sexual interest in adults, the regressed sex offenders retreat from problematic adult sexual relationships to seek emotional and physical fulfilment in a sexual relationship with a child. They project their adult needs and expectations onto their victims with the result that the children are expected to forsake childhood and become pseudo-adults.

The following case history shows how normal intimacy needs not being met can contribute to sexual abuse:

Henry was single and in his late twenties. When he first attended for treatment, he was overwhelmed by grief at the ending of his relationship with the fifteen-year-old boy with whom he had been having a sexual relationship for over a year. In Henry's eyes, it had been a relationship first and foremost, and he was unable to cope with the fact that through his sexual abuse of the boy, he had lost the relationship.

Through his writing (as part of his therapy), he showed painful insight into how he had become a sex abuser. He was an only child and lived in a remote area. Asthma further hindered him from mixing with other children and also affected his attendance at school. He described how, in the absence of playmates, he withdrew into himself, creating his own games. In secondary school, he described himself as being shy and lacking in confidence. He said that he liked girls but was too shy to talk to them. He also believed that no girl would want to have anything to do with him because of his asthma. Henry left school when he was sixteen and he became even more lonely.

He recalled how between the ages of seventeen and eighteen, his greatest pleasure was playing board games with his eight- and nine-year-old cousins, but as they grew older, they were no longer interested in coming to visit him. His parents both died when he was in his twenties, and he then lived alone in the family home. He applied to several dating agencies in an attempt to find a partner but was rejected, and he believed that he had no hope of ever having the sort of close relationship with another person that he wanted.

It was at this stage that James, the boy he later abused, started to come to his house to help him build a wall around it, a wall which Henry, with great insight, described as being like a symbolic shell that he wanted to put around himself in order to feel secure. Henry found himself looking forward more and more to James's visits, and he described how he spent his time looking out the window and waiting for him to arrive. He said he was very worried, that, like his cousins, James would go away and he would have 'no company' again. He believed that if James became close enough to him he would stay, and it was with this in mind that he initiated him into sexual activity. He believed that in this way James became more than just a friend, and that they had a real relationship. Henry regarded the sexual activity as mutual as he had never coerced or forced James to do anything. In his eyes, it was an equal relationship.

However, as the months progressed, Henry said that he became more and more dissatisfied with the relationship and he kept wishing that James was a girl. He grew jealous of the time that James spent with other people, and there were frequent rows. Henry described the situation as 'not being able to live with him or without him'. He was terrified that James would leave him and that he would be on his own again. When James was eventually able to extract himself from the relationship and tell someone what had happened, it was Henry's nightmare come true. He was forced to see the abusive nature of the relationship which he had so idealised. In addition, he had to deal with the anger of James's parents and the legal consequences of his actions. However, the hardest thing which he had to bear was being alone again, and he insisted that it was James's company rather than the sex which he missed.

The so-called regressed, non-fixated offender may also be labelled as a 'compensatory' sex offender. The offender compensates for relationship failure, real or imagined, or for an inability to adjust to or come to terms with life-stage dilemmas by projecting inappropriate relationship demands onto a child. He uses defence mechanisms to enable him to ignore the reality of his sexually abusive behaviour, and to enable him to repeat it.

These defensive mechanisms (some of which are outlined in chapter 1 in relation to how children also deny that the abuse is occurring) become part of the abuse cycle.

They include:

1   Minimising: This plays down the seriousness of the abuse, e.g. 'I was just fooling around.'
2   Rationalisation (excuses): This is an attempt on the part of the abuser to provide a plausible explanation for his behaviour, e.g. 'I was just explaining the facts of life.'
3   Projection (blaming): 'It was her fault, she was always sitting on my knee.'
4   Repression: This is a 'forgetting' of important details of the abusive behaviour which enables him to cope with the guilt, and to go on offending, e.g. blotting out the child's response, if the child is frightened.
5   Denial: As outlined in the cycle of abuse, this is the reluctance to accept the wrongness of the behaviour.

When they first come into treatment, these offenders continue to use the defence mechanisms outlined above. Through treatment, they learn to take responsibility for the fact that they targeted a child as an easier option than seeking emotional and sexual fulfilment in adult relationships. They have to come to accept that they use their positions of trust or adult authority to control their victims. It is often the exertion of that control which compensated them for the perceived loss of power with adult females.

The following case history shows how a combination of an abusive childhood, poor self-esteem and an inability to establish or maintain intimate relations contributed to one man's transformation from loving husband to child abuser:

Gerry was in his thirties, married but separated. He is very typical of the regressed, non-fixated or compensatory offender with whom we have worked; his background is depressingly familiar to us. He was one of eight children, and was unable to recall any happy memories from his childhood. His father was a heavy drinker, and the children lived in dread of his drunken return from the pub. He would drag them out of their beds and beat them with a leather belt to punish them for some alleged misdemeanour. Gerry described his mother's role as being that of a peacemaker, but she was unable to protect them from his father's rages. He felt that his father singled him out more than the others for punishment, and this physical abuse continued right up until he left home to get married.

Gerry had high hopes that his marriage would be very different from that of his parents. For a few years it seemed to be fine and he and his wife had two children. Gerry then discovered that his wife was having a relationship with another man, and he was devastated by this. He felt cheated and sexually rejected, and initially tried to get his wife to end the relationship by threatening her and bullying her (tactics which he later realised he had learned very well from his father). When this did not work, Gerry drank more and more heavily and the marriage became increasingly violent. His wife eventually left, taking the children with her.

Gerry continued to drink heavily, and wallowed in feelings of self-pity. After his separation, he spent a lot of time in his brother's house at weekends, and his twelve-year-old niece, Marie, was constantly there. Gerry missed his own family and enjoyed 'messing around' with his brother's children. Marie was always happy to see him and enjoyed the fun. Gerry is adamant that the first time he became sexually aroused when engaging in 'horseplay' with Marie, he was taken aback. However, when he next visited her, he engaged in the horseplay and became sexually aroused by it. Gerry claimed that for some time, no one else would have been aware of what was happening as the abuse was so subtle that even Marie would not have seen anything different in his behaviour towards her. But as time progressed, Gerry looked forward more and more to his contact with Marie, and he became sexually aroused whenever she appeared. He increasingly found excuses to be alone with her, and the abuse became more serious.

The fact that Marie continued to play with him and that she did not tell anyone what he was doing for a long time enabled him to engage fully in defence mechanisms which allowed him to continue abusing her.

He had for a long time minimised his abuse by describing it as 'horseplay'. He chose to forget the techniques which he was using to seduce Marie slowly into the abusive relationship. He made what he was doing to her the price which she had to pay for the continuing attention and the special relationship. He succeeded in confusing her in her understanding of what was play and part of a game and what was wrong. He did not consider what he was doing to be abuse; abuse was his father dragging him from his bed and thrashing him with a leather belt.

HOW DOES A CYCLE OF ABUSE, COGNITIVE DISTORTIONS (TWISTED THINKING) AND A LACK OF EMPATHY CONTRIBUTE TO SEX OFFENDING?

I have looked at how problems in forming intimate relationships and problems with self-image and social skills contribute to sex offending. We now need to look more closely at what is known as a cycle of abuse which is common to many of the non-fixated regressed offenders we work with.

Children elicit strong emotional responses in many adults, and these responses are usually labelled as 'affectionate' or 'protective', but they are also potentially sexual. Research has shown that normal males show some sexual arousal to female child stimuli.[16] The turning point occurs when this level of arousal becomes sufficiently high to reach consciousness. This can occur during normal adult–child interactions, bringing the child to the toilet, bathing the child, tucking him/her into bed, or engaging in 'horseplay'. The adult must define the physiological arousal he is experiencing as being sexual and as being elicited by the child before the possibility arises of the experience being used as a masturbatory fantasy. If this happens, and if it is combined with the fact that the man, for various reasons, does not use normal adult sexual activity as the content of his fantasy, a dangerous pattern emerges. The man will then indulge solely in fantasies of sexual activity with a child as an aid to masturbation.

As a result of what offenders report to us, we believe that their exclusive use of sexual fantasies involving a child as an aid to masturbation leads them to act out that fantasy and to sexually abuse a child. The abuse cycle can be summarised as follows:[17]

- The adult experiences sexual arousal in relation to a child.
- He uses the recall of this experience as the content of his sexual fantasy, which results in masturbation.
- He continues to do this, often for many months, and the fantasy involving sexual activity with the child becomes his only source of sexual arousal.
- He targets a child and focuses on creating the conditions in which he can act out his fantasy.
- He grooms the child.
- He abuses the child.
- He experiences fear and guilt afterwards, and thinks 'I'll never do it again.'
- He uses distorted thinking to make himself feel better about what he has done, e.g. 'It was only horseplay.'
- The child does not tell, and his anxiety recedes.
- He starts to use the recall of the abuse of the child as the basis of his sexual fantasy and masturbation.
- He will distort and repress the nature of the abuse to allow him to do this, e.g. 'She did not tell, she must have enjoyed it.'
- Above all, he will engage in denial, i.e. an inability to accept that the sexual behaviour he indulged in is harmful to the victim, is not desired by her, and is in fact criminal and coercive.

The above summary, while dealing with the main steps which

lead from potentially dangerous fantasies to abuse, is of necessity simplistic. The reality, when we work closely with individuals, is more complex. In particular, the men we work with are seldom aware that they are targeting or 'grooming' a child. These terms imply that what happens is a deliberate, calculated, carefully determined act. In practice, what commonly happens is much more opportunistic. The child who is abused is very often abused for no other reason than that she is available. The relationship which the offender builds up with the child may appear to him to be so reciprocal that he is unable to see it as grooming. The child may deliberately seek out the company of the offender, and obviously enjoy the time that they spend together. It is often difficult for the offender to pinpoint when the boundaries within the relationship become blurred and love turns to lust. He will certainly often not see himself as having deliberately encouraged the relationship with the child in order to abuse her.

This is why a lot of the work done in treatment focuses on what happened in the offender's life before and at the time when he formed the relationship with the child. He needs to understand what emotional needs the relationship with the child met for him, and to take full responsibility for his abuse of the child's right to have a loving relationship with an adult.

In addition to the above cycle of abuse, there are other factors which contribute to the abuse happening. These are that the offender has the motivation to abuse, that he can overcome his own internal inhibitions and other, external inhibitions, and finally that he can overcome the resistance of the child.[18]

In terms of motivation, there is often a blockage whereby other sources of sexual and emotional gratification are unavailable or less satisfying. An emotional need to relate intimately with someone is coupled with a sexual interest in children which then leads to abuse.

The second prerequisite is that the offender overcomes the normal internal inhibitions which exist to prevent the breaking of this taboo. He does this by distorting the nature of his behaviour to himself (cognitive distortion) or by abusing alcohol. The offender must also overcome the external inhibitors, such as the supervision of the child by others. Finally, he must overcome the resistance of the child by building trust, using blackmail or physical force.

Treatment involves these preconditions being outlined, and each offender identifying how each one relates to him. This exercise is done both verbally in the group, to enable the men to confront each other, and in written form, to reinforce the important insights they gain into their individual offence cycle.

The following case history shows how sexual abuse occurs as a result of the offender's multiple deficits, and that it is not adequate in treatment to focus only on the sexual offending behaviour.

Daniel, an immature man in his twenties, described how, before his offence, he felt that he was useless and 'not worth a damn'. He attributed these feelings to his inability, in spite of his good looks, to have a girlfriend for any length of time. He had had numerous short-term girlfriends but they all gave him a similar story about really liking him as a friend but not wanting to have a relationship with him. Daniel blamed his mother for this situation. He described how when he brought a girlfriend home, his mother would interrogate her in a very aggressive manner, and how the girls 'beat a hasty retreat'. Daniel felt that his mother had no confidence in his ability to pick a girlfriend, and that she considered none of the girls good enough for him. He was angry with himself that he was not able to stand up to his mother, and angry with the girlfriends that they gave up on him so quickly.

He was seething inside, but appeared a 'cool, happy-go-lucky' person to the outside world. He felt that he had no refuge, and nobody who he could be himself with. He pretended to his friends at work that he was not bothered by his lack of a girlfriend, and he was too afraid to challenge his mother openly.

It was with Caroline, the eight-year-old girl who lived next door, that he felt most at ease. She seemed to look out for him coming home from work, and even if she was outside playing with friends, she left them and came running over to talk to

him. He spent as much time as possible with her, especially during the summer holidays.

Daniel identified the first incident which changed the relationship as being when he went behind a bush to urinate and
Caroline innocently wandered up and stood watching him. He
explained in treatment how he found himself thinking about the
incident, and feeling sexually aroused by it.

It can be seen from this case study how the factor of motivation to abuse developed. The relationship with Caroline met
Daniel's emotional needs of feeling wanted and appreciated.
Other sources of sexual and emotional gratification were problematic for him as a result of his mother's dominance, and his
fearfulness and the accidental exposure of his penis to Caroline
became a source of sexual arousal.

It was at this stage that Daniel had the responsibility to draw
back and resist exploiting the relationship he had with Caroline.
In hindsight, he recognised that he first crossed a crucial boundary line when he allowed Caroline to remain watching while he
finished urinating. However, when he next had an opportunity,
he asked the child if she would like to see his penis again. In this
way, the sexual abuse of Caroline by Daniel began, and it progressed gradually to more serious abuse.

Daniel overcame the normal 'internal inhibitions' by increasing the level of the abuse very slowly, and by carrying it out
within the context of the loving relationship. In this way, he also
overcame Caroline's resistance by making it their special secret,
and rewarding her compliance with lots of attention and sweets.
Thus, he was able to distort the nature of his behaviour to himself
by telling himself that since Caroline chose to come with him,
and since she did not tell anyone what he was doing, it was not
harmful to her.

When Daniel's twisted thinking was confronted, it emerged
that Caroline had not liked what he was doing to her and had
asked him to stop. He had responded to this by stopping for a
short while and then gradually overcoming her resistance again.

Daniel had no difficulty in overcoming 'external inhibitors' such as the supervision of Caroline by her family. He was from a respectable family, friendly with her parents, and as Caroline was one of a large family, she was scarcely missed when she spent time with him. In fact, Daniel claimed that her family were pleased that he had taken such an interest in her.

It is understandable how the offenders themselves stress that parents are not vigilant enough about where their children are, who they are with, and what they are doing. It is this that facilitates the abuse of a young and trusting child, like Caroline, by an offender like Daniel. In this case, the abuse continued for over two years.

THE FAMILY THERAPY APPROACH TO UNDERSTANDING SEXUAL ABUSE

Also known as the systemic approach, the family therapy approach is a very effective way of acknowledging the complexities of the relationships within a family in which sexual abuse occurs.[19] These complexities are often ignored in the simplistic response of legislators, judiciary, media and so on, who presume that it is enough to rescue the victim and punish the abuser and all will be well.

Within the systemic framework, the power of the offending behaviour and the part it plays in stabilising family life is acknowledged. This does not mean that the sexually abusive behaviour is not the sole responsibility of the abuser. Rather, it acknowledges that issues which involve the individual also extend to the family and the wider social context. As feminist researchers have documented very well, women and children have traditionally been expected to endure high levels of abuse.[20]

The nature of the relationships within the family itself is viewed as often reflecting how the abusive experiences of the parents in their own families are re-created and re-enacted in their current family – living out the old folk wisdom that 'the apple does not fall far from the tree'.

There is a lot of debate about what is described as the

'interlocking roles' in sexual abuse within families.[21] Questions raised include whether men who sexually abuse their children 'find' vulnerable partners, or are found by partners who have themselves been abused; and whether there is a complementary 'fit' of perpetrator and victim.

In one study, 43 per cent of the mothers of children who were abused had themselves been abused in childhood, and up to 30 per cent of the fathers who had abused.[22] Both the abusers and the mothers are described as having had 'very mixed care' in childhood, and many of them had few good memories of this time. Over one-third of the mothers could not bring themselves to believe that their children had been abused by their partners, and they supported the parent who denied responsibility rather than believe the child.

In many cases, violence is an integral part of family life which society implicitly accepts through its lack of condemnation. Over time, different members of the family become either aggressor or victim in a dynamic that remains unknown to or ignored by the wider community.

In reality, the health of a family system bears no relationship to its public image or to whether the family regards what is happening within it to be normal. The conspicuously abusive family, in which there is obvious alcoholism, poverty, neglect, and with whom social services are likely to be involved, represents only a small percentage of all abusive families. Most families in which sexual abuse occurs fit well into the community. Even if such a family is not well regarded, it is seen as being of a particular type, and few questions are asked about what happens behind closed doors.

Through a process of denial, incest in a family is sometimes viewed as an attempt to preserve family functioning and balance in the family unit. Characteristics frequently observed in families in which incest occurs are summarised as follows:[23]

1   There is pervasive denial by all family members about incest or addiction.

2 The situation is not how the individual family member per-
ceives it but how the family defines the situation or says that
it is.

3 There is isolation from the community.

4 All problems are denied.

5 There is a lack of clear boundaries and rules.

6 There is triangulation between mother, father and child – it
becomes the child's responsibility to maintain the family,
and frequently the parents have a dysfunctional sexual
relationship.

7 There is little acceptance of anger, conflict and deviations from
what is considered the norm in the family.

8 There is a rigidity in religious beliefs (e.g. the child is taught
that it is a sin to engage in premarital sexual activities; meanwhile the father sexually abuses her).

9 Touching that is non-sexual and genuinely loving and nurturing is non-existent.

10 Children's emotional and other physical needs are ignored.

11 Emotional abuse is rampant, and children are often humiliated
and shamed.

12 Parents are withdrawn and emotionally and physically unavailable; one or both parents may be addicted to work or
alcohol.

13 Children are unwanted and are treated as such.

14 There are rampant inconsistencies in the treatment of the child
– behaviour that is acceptable one day may be unacceptable
the next.

15 There are threats of violence which are sometimes carried out.

16 The child is isolated with no one to tell, and so deals with the
situation the best she knows how. This may be by disassociation, or, in cases where the abuse is extreme, she may develop
multiple personality disorder as a surviving mechanism. (See
chapter 1.)

There are 'overt' and 'covert' systems which operate in abusive families.[24] These two systems operate simultaneously but
independently of one another. The 'overt' system is made up of
everyday activities like meals, television watching, household

chores, bedtime rituals and family celebrations. The family members bond to each other at this level. They care for each other and have an image of their family as normal. The 'covert' system contains 'the secrets, the shame, the weaknesses, the hidden hopes and dreams, and the deepest emotional forces that sweep through the family'.

This is the level of family life that no one talks about but everyone senses. Sexual abuse occurs at this covert level of family functioning. It is a secret which has tremendous impact on the family but which is hidden from the outside world. Family members may or may not be consciously aware of the abuse, but even if they do know about it, they do not speak about it. Everyone knows when to disappear, what not to question, and when to look away. In this way, several members of the same family may be sexually abused by the parent but never discuss this with each other. The greater the discrepancy between the overt system and the covert system, the greater the likelihood that the victim will choose to repress or 'forget' her sexual abuse. The child often has difficulty in reconciling the parent who is good to them at other times and bad only during the sexual abuse. If, in addition, the parent is popular and respected in the community, the pressure to 'forget' about the abuse is even stronger.

Sexual abuse within a family is evidence of family dysfunction. But families do not exist in isolation. They have their own context – their extended family and friends, the neighbourhood and the wider social and political setting.

In family therapy, child abuse is understood not only through what happens between the offender and the victim and their interactions with the rest of the family, but through the interactions of the family within its own specific context, including its interactions with the wider social network.

The systemic approach to intervention in such families aims first to disrupt the process of denial and silencing.[25] This is followed by an assessment of the whole family, not just the offenders. The capacity of families to respond to treatment is assessed as 'hopeful', 'doubtful' or 'hopeless' depending upon the degree to which the offender accepts responsibility for the abuse, the non-abusing parent accepts responsibility for failing to protect the victim, and the family shows a capacity to engage in treatment.

Intervention in families assessed as 'hopeful' and 'doubtful' involves individual and group treatment for the offender (in addition to him receiving any legal sanctions), and individual or group therapy for the victim or victims, the other children in the family and the non-abusing parent. All the individuals affected by the abuse receive treatment in various combinations. For instance, the offender attends a re-education and training programme; the victim, the other children and the non-abusing parent receive counselling. Family work is carried out initially in dyads – for example, parents together; victim with the non-abusing, supportive parent; and victim with brother or sister.[26] The final stage of intervention is the reunification of the family in a very gradual way, if and when it is considered safe for the victim and the offender to live together again.

The following case study illustrates some of the characteristics of families in which abuse occurs and the complexities of the interwoven relationships in a family.

When Margaret Doherty told one of her teachers that her father 'was having sex' with her, a door was forced open which shed light on what was happening behind the façade of normality in her family. Margaret was the youngest of four girls, aged between eighteen and thirteen. Her parents, Kevin and Carmel, were a 'normal' couple in their forties. Kevin worked in the building trade and Carmel remained at home on the small farm in the remote rural area where the family had lived for the previous eight years.

The true extent of this family's isolation and Kevin's control over them emerged during the investigation which followed Margaret's disclosure. Kevin and Carmel's 'marriage' was significant in the enabling of the covert system to exist. Carmel had originally been married to a cousin of Kevin's but had left this marriage after six months and 'run off' with Kevin. This resulted in their isolation from their disapproving families, both described by Carmel as being 'rough and tough'. They had settled in a large town and the girls were born there. However, Kevin then moved his family to the farm, where they lived in a two-bedroomed cottage in poor circumstances.

Kevin was a heavy drinker and the family was constantly short of money. He was never violent or openly aggressive but he was very dominant and dictated the rules of the family. The girls travelled to school by bus each day and were not allowed to take part in any activities outside of school or to have any friends. They were expected to help with work on the farm at their father's bidding. The pattern which Margaret described was one of her father asking her to help him outside and then sexually abusing her in an old caravan directly beside the house.

When Margaret's sisters were interviewed, Karen, the eldest, admitted that her father had sexually abused her for a number of years but she was critical rather than supportive of Margaret, saying, 'When I told him to stop [having sex with me], he did.' She also refused to make a statement to the police about her father. While the professionals involved were convinced that the other two girls had also been abused, they denied this.

Carmel was very ambivalent. As Kevin admitted the abuse, she had no choice but to believe Margaret. However, she minimised what Kevin had done and initially refused to accept that the sexual abuse had involved intercourse. Her dilemma was evident in her statement: 'I gave up everything for him.' It appeared that this, combined with Kevin's manipulative isolation and domination of the family, was enough to prevent her from protecting the children.

The three older sisters sided with their mother. Kevin was seen as the victim who had to leave the family home and Carmel and the three girls did everything to make life easier for him. Margaret was isolated within the family and made to feel responsible for her father being out of the house. The other girls also resented the extra work they had to do on the farm as a result of their father's absence.

Margaret's three sisters chose to avail of supervised access to their father. The professionals observing the family noted how all touching was sexual and there was no evidence of any genuinely loving and nurturing touch – one of the characteristics of abusive families. Kevin and his daughters greeted each other with inappropriate close physical embraces and mouth kissing. Apart from this initial greeting, there was little communication between them; in fact, the girls asked for a television in the access room in order to pass the time.

While the prognosis for this family appeared 'doubtful', long-term intervention over a number of years has considerably improved their level of well-being. Kevin was given a suspended sentence on condition that he attend a re-education and training programme. This he did, under the close supervision of the probation and welfare service. There, he underwent all of the treatment components outlined in the appendix, which resulted in him taking responsibility for his abusive behaviour and recognising the harm it did to his daughters.

Margaret received counselling and support to enable her to cope not just with the sexual abuse but with the impact of her disclosure. Carmel needed intensive intervention to deal with issues from her own past, her lack of self-esteem and her dependency on Kevin to assist her to become a more protective parent. Work was also done with Carmel and Margaret together to attempt to repair the damage done by Carmel's colluding with Kevin. With the other girls, the aim was to reduce the blame they placed on Margaret and to develop their capacity to protect themselves. Carmel and Kevin also worked on their own relationship during this time and it became much more equal and challenging.

The family was eventually reunited after a number of years and there is continuing contact with the child protection services.

In this chapter, various theories have been explored which contribute to our understanding as to why adults sexually abuse children. What we learn from all of them is that it is inadequate in our preventative work to focus on the sexual offending behaviour alone. The multiple deficits which enable individuals to become sex offenders require a comprehensive response in the contents of re-education and training programmes. Therapists have to assess the contribution of each theory to their understanding of the behaviour of the individual offender before them and then devise the interventions best suited to reduce the risk of him reoffending.

7

Sexual abuse and the media
How myths and half-truths
are perpetuated

The language we use to describe or define problems has a huge effect on how we, as a society, respond to and deal with such problems. Myths and stereotypes of sexual abuse are often perpetuated by the overuse and misuse of terms in the media. Various commonly used words carry underlying meanings which I believe are emotive and limiting to the individuals they describe. I would first like to draw attention to these terms before discussing in more detail how myths and half-truths about sexual abuse are continually repeated and reinforced by the media.

Take for example the word *victim*. This is a very emotive term whose emphasis is on passivity and powerlessness. While it may be an accurate view of the person's state at the time of the abuse, it should not imply that they are permanently 'fixed' in that role. (See also chapter 8.) *Survivor* is another unfortunate term as it implies that the trauma is ongoing and, as such, incapacitates the abused person to the extent that they 'will never be the same again' or that their 'lives are completely destroyed'. While the trauma of abuse must in no way be minimised, the use of limiting reductionist terminology may encourage a patronising attitude on the part of non-abused persons and limit overall expectations of recovery. It may also limit our capacity to encourage, support and evoke more positive self-healing responses from the abused person.

The term *offender* is misleading in that it is too general. Here, the emphasis is on criminality with little acknowledgement of the complexity of the problem or, indeed, our own contribution to the problem through our indifference. *Perpetrator* has implications of planning and of being in full control of one's actions. While in some respects abusers do work out a strategy of abuse, the term does not include any consideration of the preceding life events which contributed to the development of this mind-set.

The idea of an *offender profile* is likewise often inappropriate. It suggests that offenders have certain characteristics which can be recognised and which can be used to identify such persons. The reality is that most offenders are 'normal' members of society and are not usually suspect until their abusive behaviour is disclosed.

In the absence of an alternative vocabulary, we continue to use these terms. It is, however, important that we do so with a full awareness of their limitations. Both offenders and victims are members of our society and what we say about them also applies to us. We have to ask ourselves in what ways we are victims and/or offenders and to what extent we have contributed to the abusive behaviour and twisted thinking which resulted in sexual abuse. A classic example of twisted thinking in the professional context is the professional's approach to sexual abuse. By being detached from the problem, professionals believe that they are somehow immune from faulty perceptions or that, because they are 'qualified', 'trained' or in some way 'expert', they will never abuse or be abused emotionally. This is not always the case and sexual abuse by professional carers of children has come to light over the last decade.

Terminology aside, journalists must also question themselves on the issue of the responsibility they uphold on our behalf. We have all witnessed adult victims of sexual abuse being further 'abused' by intrusive voyeuristic questioning on radio and television chat shows. The questions which they are most repeatedly and persistently asked are 'What did he do?' and 'What did he do then?' In the pseudo-intimacy of the radio or television studio, victims are persuaded to reveal to the nation the most distressing physical details of their abuse under the guise of public interest. How much are the interests of the victims being served when national newspapers outline horrific details of their abuse? And are we really learning more about sexual abuse through such interviews? Does such stark and often insensitive reporting of sexual abuse ever help to prevent further abuse from happening?

Other media portrayals of victims rely heavily on a mixture of dramatic visual images, for example a doll breaking in slow motion, and the use of mood music to create dramatic effects which distract from the realness of the stories to be told. The RTÉ *Tuesday File* (1995) portrayal of the Kavanagh sisters, all of whom were sexually abused by their father for many years, was an exception to this intrusive style of interviewing and noteworthy for this reason. These women were ordinary individuals telling the story of their abuse in a straightforward, non-dramatic way. This one programme did much more to educate the Irish public about the apparent normality of a family in which abuse occurs than all the efforts to turn the topic of sexual abuse into a mixture of high drama and horror story.

Denial is often spoken of in relation to abusers. Why should it be tacitly assumed that everyone else is exempt from denials? To argue that sexual abusers must be punished when we know that the legal process is not victim-friendly and that treatment facilities in prison are in many respects inadequate is another form of denial. To focus on the abuser as if he did not exist prior to the disclosure of the abuse and as if there are no other aspects to his life is also a form of denial. Yet another form of denial is to claim that child sexual abuse is a major problem and then to respond as though the only solution is the imposition of the full rigour of the law.

We hear these denials all the time in the media and from pressure groups and fellow professionals who focus on the problem in a narrow reductionist manner.

The treatment of abusers by the media has been uniform in its portrayal of the abusers as 'all evil'. Profiles of the abuser are presented involving targeting, manipulation, bribery, coercion and so on, as if all abusers were exactly the same. This prevents us from seeing them as individuals, and makes it extremely difficult to judge their actions on a case-by-case basis.

Little media coverage is given to the cycle of abuse and the fact that some abusers have themselves been the victims of sexual abuse. While this is never to be taken as an excuse for their abusive behaviour, it does pose a challenge to our perception of the victims, and our conditional acceptance of them.

Television often visually presents sex offenders as dark shadowy silhouettes with distorted voices, or – as in one interview with an offender – close-up shots of different parts of the face are shown to grotesque effect. While there are obvious difficulties in persuading sex abusers to speak openly on camera, such presentation serves only to perpetuate the demonising of the abusers, and create a 'them and us' situation.

There appears to be little compunction on the part of the media about respecting the rights of sex offenders. The men who take part in the offenders' treatment programme with which I am involved were asked to contribute to a television programme on sex abuse. Those who agreed to do so were among the most insightful and most remorseful of the group. They saw their participation in the programme as an opportunity to repay some of their debt both to their victims and to society. They had important things to say about how to prevent the sexual abuse of children and the value of treatment. In particular, they wanted to encourage other sex offenders who might be watching to stop abusing and to seek treatment. The makers assured the men full anonymity. In addition, they were told that they would be shown the completed programme before it was transmitted.

The men co-operated fully. However, neither of these agreements was honoured. They were not shown the completed programme. They were shown in silhouette but their voices were not disguised and were easily recognisable in their local areas; one man was physically attacked as a result. (The only reason offered for this breach of agreement by the programme makers was that someone had pushed the 'wrong button!')

The most serious betrayal of these men, however, was in the editing of what they had said. Only statements which presented them in an unfavourable and negative light were broadcast. These statements were interwoven with interviews with adult victims in a very emotive way. Needless to say, any further requests to the men to talk to the media were unsuccessful.

Sex offenders, as well as their victims, suffer at the hands of the media when the details of their offences are published – particularly when the offender can also be named and photographed. Questions need to be asked about the often disturbing level of detail published in relation to sexual abuse cases. How much in the public interest are such articles which further abuse the victim and punish the offender?

In Sweden, where the society is deemed to be one of the most open in the world, criminal proceedings in the courts are not reported unless coverage is deemed to be in the public interest.[1] The rationale for this voluntary policy is threefold. It is based on a belief that publicity amounts to an additional punishment not envisaged by law; that publicity can injure innocent third parties (family members, victims); and that publicity makes the task of rehabilitating the offender more difficult.

My work with sex offenders and victims and the families of both bears witness to the truth of these three points. Sex offenders in particular are seen as being 'fair game' for hunting and harrying in order to provide the sensational story, a point illustrated by this case history.

Peter, a respected professional who successfully completed

treatment, lost everything as a result of the disclosure of his sexual abuse of a child ten years previously. He lost his job, his income, his home, his hobbies and most of his friends. He was unusual in terms of the men who attend for treatment as he had stopped his sexual abuse of the child because of his own awareness of the wrongness of what he was doing. He was given a suspended prison sentence by the court but the media exacted their own punishment, carrying his photograph, interviews with his now adult victim and the details of his abuse. In addition, his family, friends and ex-colleagues were hounded by journalists all looking for a sensational scoop.

We have to question the values of a society which is so eager to use sex offenders as scapegoats, and to condemn one type of abuse but not another. Scapegoating of offenders also occurs at a local level, before the alleged perpetrator is ever found guilty by the courts. This is often done with no thought for its impact on the victim, whom everyone purports to be concerned about. The following case history puts this point in perspective.

Brian's teenage niece rather reluctantly disclosed that the very close relationship she had with him had become sexual. The young girl had mixed feelings about revealing this as like many victims, she believed that she was responsible for what had happened. She was also very fond of her uncle. Within a short time of her disclosure, Brian's work colleagues started to make life unbearable for him. Their secondary abuse of him was subtle and effective. Nobody spoke to him. He was moved to a position where he had to deal directly with the very hostile local public. On a number of occasions, he was allowed just enough time to get home, a one-hour drive away, before being recalled to his workplace, particularly when road conditions were dangerous. The situation became intolerable and he felt he had no choice but to resign from his job. The local news-sheet also headlined the accusations made against him and while he was not named, enough information was given to enable him to be easily identified in his local area.

All of this was deeply distressing to his already ambivalent victim. She bitterly regretted her disclosure when she saw the consequences for her uncle and the anguish and hurt caused to her extended family.

In this situation, society is using the trauma of the victim to impose its own concepts of justice. Much of our experience over the years has indicated that often the victim, on whose behalf we all purport to speak, is consulted only to the extent that the offender is identified.

The victim's disclosure of abuse – rather than empowering her – takes the process of ending the abuse, and restoring her health and wholeness, out of her hands. An official response is implemented which takes no account of the complexities of the situation. Hence all abusers are bad and must be punished, not treated, and victims have to be 'rescued' and protected irrespective of their wishes, and of the consequences for them and their families. (See chapter 3.)

In reality no two cases of sexual abuse are alike. We need the media to reflect more accurately the complexities surrounding abuse and society's response to it. The high-profile cases need to be reported within the broader context of the overall prevalence and pervasiveness of the abuse of children in our society.

One commentator queries the 'rituals of astonishment and shock' in response to the reporting of such cases.[2] He refers to one survey in which one in eight Irish adults indicated that they had been sexually abused in childhood. From this he speculates on the large number of people in the population who have some knowledge of sex abuse – the victims, the perpetrators and the intimate friends of the victims – and concludes that sex abuse is deeply ingrained in normal life. However, the media do little to close what is described as 'the gap between what we know and what we are prepared to believe'. The hard cases make good copy and sell papers.

It is an unpalatable fact of life that extreme perversion and cruelty do manifest themselves in the existence of paedophile rings and in barbaric acts such as the child murders in Belgium. This has to be reported and acted on. However, if most publicity is only about the extreme cases of abuse, it makes it easier for the public not to 'believe what is known'. Many victims in turn believe that their experiences are insignificant when the definitions of abuse become paired with the extremes of depravity. This often results in such victims remaining silent and then not being able to come to terms fully with what happened to them and move on in their lives.

8

Living with the experience of sexual abuse
What makes some victims cope better than others

> 'I've got all my life to live,
> I've got all my love to give,
> I will survive.'
> Gloria Gaynor

There is no doubt that all childhood sexual abuse is damaging to victims. Even those victims who appear to cope well at the time may encounter difficulties related to the abuse later on in life. The well-recognised problems resulting from the experience of sexual abuse include the betrayal of trust, the interruption of sexual development, and a confusion of roles.[1]

The recent practice of providing victim impact statements to help the judge determine appropriate sentencing is a very welcome one. However, these reports are prepared at a time of great stress for the victim. (See chapter 3.) I am concerned that victims are invariably portrayed in media reporting of such cases as passive and helpless, 'their lives ruined' by the abuse. Such a portrayal is at odds with the complexities of individuals' stories and the numerous factors which help victims to overcome the damaging effects of abuse. It is also detrimental to all victims, past and present, who, in addition to having to deal with the victim label at the time the abuse is disclosed, are also faced with the bleak future of being victims for ever.

This 'victim for ever' myth has been nurtured by the media and professionals and even by women's groups, who originally brought the problem to public attention. In a cameo in the film *Single White Female*, an obviously neurotic woman declares, as part of her self-description, that she is a survivor – of what exactly she is not sure, but she just knows that she is. This light moment highlights the more serious issue that being a survivor of childhood sexual abuse has become a status symbol.

The disclosure by well-known personalities such as Roseanne Barr, LaToya Jackson and Sinéad O'Connor of their abusive childhood has contributed to a disturbing trend which denigrates the anguish of those who suffer in silence. In the United States in particular, being an abuse survivor has become an important identity. The prominent American researcher and writer on such issues, David Finkelhor, suggests that 'sexual identity has to some extent replaced family identity even as the way people locate themselves in the social matrix'.[2] Instead of working through private grief, some personalities who go public on abuse use the myth of the permanently destroyed victim as the explanation for all that is wrong in their lives.

This oversimplified view of the long-term effects of sexual abuse has become prevalent in the past decade. Healthcare professionals have sat through conferences and read numerous studies in which virtually every conceivable psychiatric and social problem experienced by individuals has been attributed to childhood sexual abuse. A lot of this research focused on what are known as single factor studies. Researchers tested problematic adult populations to see if an unusually large number of individuals within these subgroups had been sexually abused. Many of them had and a mind-set developed among researchers that the discovery of sexual abuse explained practically everything.

Psychiatric problems, depression and anxiety, eating disorders, sexual difficulties, substance abuse and so on have all been found to be related to sexual abuse. This led to what has been described by Finkelhor as a 'one size fits all treatment mentality' and a 'cherchez l'abuse' approach, followed by the assumption that, if the abuse experience is worked through, all will be well in the individuals' lives again.

It is now understood that the picture is much more complex than this. The focus on sexual abuse in much research arose in part from the need to counteract the resistance of both professionals and the public to accepting its existence. I believe that this strong advocacy mentality on the part of those wishing to highlight the existence of sexual abuse, and the damage caused by it, has outlived its usefulness. It is now oversimplistic and in danger of doing a disservice to many victims for whom the concentration on sexual abuse to the exclusion of other relevant life factors is detrimental to their recovery. It also leads to victims being disempowered and inhibits their belief in their own potential to grow and to move on from surviving to thriving.

One of the questions that needs to be answered in this new analysis of the effects of sexual abuse is why some children are less damaged than others by the experience of sexual abuse. Here, we need to look at two types of effects which result from all forms of victimisation, including sexual abuse. These effects are either localised (i.e. those which occur immediately after the abuse or are linked directly to the abusive situation) and/or developmental (i.e. those which damage the psychological and sometimes even the physical development of the individual over a longer period).[3]

Localised effects refer to the common post-traumatic symptoms, which are often short-term. These behaviours are associated with the experience of being victimised. They include fearfulness, fear of returning to the place where the abuse occurred, anxiety around adults who resemble the abuser, nightmares and other anxiety symptoms.

In contrast, developmental effects are deeper and have a much more generalised and long-term impact on the individual. These include damaged attachment to significant adults, low self-esteem, highly sexualised or highly aggressive behaviour, an inability to make friends, the use of drugs and self-injury. These damaging developmental effects are more likely to occur if some of the following conditions are present:

1   The abuse is repetitive and ongoing – for example, if a child is abused over a number of years and if there is more than one abuser.[4]

2   The abuse dramatically changes the nature of the child's relationship with his main carers. Sexual abuse by a trusted family member, particularly a parent, is usually more damaging than abuse by an unfamiliar adult outside of the family.[5] The rejection of the child by parents as a result of abuse has a similar damaging effect. The child being believed and supported by the parents, or by the non-abusing parent (if the abuser is a parent), is essential in minimising the trauma; if the parents do not believe, or if they minimise the abuse or place the blame on the child for it occurring, then the negative effects of the abuse are greater.[6]

3   The sexual abuse occurs alongside other forms of abuse or traumatic life events.[7] Children who are sexually abused may also suffer from other forms of abuse, both physical and emotional, as well as inadequate parenting. Bereavement, parental separation and poor schooling will also increase the trauma of sexual abuse.

4   Because of its timing or source, the abuse interrupts a crucial development transition. Attachment to a primary caretaker, usually a parent, is considered one of the first important developmental tasks of childhood.[8] Children form attachments as soon as they are born. By three to six months the baby responds most significantly to two or three people or often to one special

person. This person will be the one who is most in tune with and most responsive to the baby. By about six months of age the baby becomes intensely attached to one person and may cry when that person leaves the room. By seven or eight months, the baby will crawl after his caretaker and hold out his arms to be picked up. When the attachment between the child and the mother figure is secure, the toddler can then begin to explore his world but continue to return to the mother when feeling afraid or when needing to check that the mother figure is still there. By the time the child reaches five years of age he will be secure in the belief that the mother figure is always there and that even if she goes away for a time, she will return. This base of secure attachment is essential for the emotional well-being of the child. It enables him to deal with separations and to enter new situations with a sense of confidence.

Children who are abused physically, emotionally or sexually at an early age by their primary caretaker seem to have insecure attachment to these individuals. This insecurity in primary relationships is often carried into later stages of development and into other relationships. A child with insecure basic attachments will be more vulnerable – both in terms of being sexually abused again and in their capacity to recover from the abuse.

Such children often feel unloved and unwanted. This leaves them prey to other abusers who offer affection, attention and treats in return for sexual activity. It must always be remembered that the child is never, ever responsible for the sexual abuse. However, emotional neediness on the part of the child or young person may cause him to view the sexual interaction as positive because it fulfils his need for feeling loved and feeling special, regardless of the fact that being abused is the price he must pay.

Children who are sexually abused during their pre-school years are at risk of being left with what are called disassociative scars in later life.[9] These include periods of derealisation (lapses into fantasy worlds), memory losses, trancelike behaviour, auditory or visual hallucinations, or, in extreme cases, multiple personalities. This is because all children of this age have a great capacity to fantasise, having imaginary playmates and being able to freely deny having done things which they had done.

For young children who have been abused the response of their parents is crucial.[10] The most important issue for the children may not be whether they think they have the power to prevent further abuse but whether they think their parents do. Also crucial is whether the cause of the abuse is constantly present across time and across situations.

Young children may not be mature enough to recognise abuse when it occurs. They do not have the knowledge of social norms, the concepts of personal rights and responsibilities or the ability to make social comparisons. However, even if a child does not recognise abuse at the time it occurs, she can realise later what happened and this brings great distress.

That the effects of abuse vary according to the age of the victim has been documented by the fact that child victims go on to show new symptoms as they mature.[11] What happens is that their changing beliefs about the abuse can affect their social lives and relationships with others. As puberty approaches, sexually abused girls may feel more isolated from their own age group. Their self-esteem may be lowered by their worries about their sexual desirability or reputation.[12] Sexually abused boys are often unwilling to disclose their abuse as they approach puberty as a result of their increased awareness of the stigma of homosexuality.[13]

Different symptoms are also specifically associated with certain age groups.[14] For example, sexualised behaviour often observed as a result of sexual abuse is most associated with two- to six-year-olds. Older girls respond to sexual abuse more with inhibition than with acting out. Among adolescents, common symptoms of abuse appear to be depression, self-injurious behaviour, running away and substance abuse.

The child's individual personality and physical appearance also influence the impact of sexual abuse.[15] Physically attractive children have been found to be less damaged because teachers often respond more favourably to attractive children. Being attractive also makes it easier for the child to form friendships. The child who is enjoying school and feeling a sense of competence in an academic, social or athletic area is less likely to have later difficulties.[16]

Having a positive relationship with their fathers has also been found to be crucially important for victims in their teenage years.[17] As most sexual abuse is perpetrated by men, the benefits of this relationship are obvious. For adolescent girls, having a good relationship with boys has a good effect on self-esteem.

Researchers also believe that severe psychological trauma can have long-lasting effects on physiological processes such as endo-crine and neurological functioning.[18]

Sexual abuse and other trauma has also been found to hasten the onset of puberty. Girls who have been sexually abused may have their periods earlier than their peer group. The more chronic and severe the abuse in terms of physical abuse or injury, the greater the developmental effects. All victims are affected more by abuse when they believe they are going to die or be seriously injured, or when they feel helpless and out of control.[19]

Sadly, for many children, sexual abuse is but one of many negative experiences in their lives.[20] These children also suffer from other forms of abuse (both physical and emotional) and in-adequate parenting. They may not have a supportive adult in their lives. Their disclosure of abuse may not be believed or may not be acted upon. The abuser may also be the parent. If they are neglected and their appearance and hygiene are poor, they will have difficulty forming relationships. Poor schooling will lead to poor attendance, leading to poor examination per-formance, leading to unemployment or low-paid unskilled work.

The psychological difficulties experienced by adult victims may therefore be caused by a constellation of negative childhood factors which precede and surround the sexual abuse. The sexual abuse trauma is mixed in with a lot of other abuses and depriva-tions. One might realise therefore that in each case of sexual abuse, as indeed in any other abusive or traumatic experience, a whole range of factors will determine the impact of the abusive behaviour.[21] These factors are often not highlighted when blanket statements are made about the impact of abuse on the individual.

It has been shown that the effects of sexual abuse, unless the abuse has been very severe, involving penetration, are far less for women who do not have other problems.[22] Women who suffered from physical abuse, neglect or other problems as well as sexual abuse (regardless of its severity) are more likely to have problems in adulthood.

Another factor which makes it more difficult to determine the impact of sexual abuse on victims is that of retraumatisation.[23] Many victims of sexual abuse seem to continue to suffer additional traumas and disabling life events that either keep the original trauma alive or add new psychological scars. Examples include the victim who goes on – after the abuse has ended – to have an unwanted pregnancy, to contract a sexually transmitted disease, to live with an abusive partner or to suffer additional sexual or physical attacks.

When adult victims present for treatment, the origins of their current problems may be much more immediate than the sexual abuse in their past. We have, over the years, learned the value of focusing on the immediate life crisis which brings the adult victim to our services rather than focusing only on their past sexual abuse. The recent crisis, such as marriage difficulties, may be related to the childhood sexual abuse in that the abuse seems to render the victims more vulnerable. However, without the additional problems, the adult victim might have been coping well with the abuse.

These life events which determine the adult victim's ability to cope with childhood sexual abuse are called mediators.[24] These mediators include all the factors in the child's life before and after the abuse, including having secure attachments, quality of parenting, the role of school, social supports, friendships and relationships.

Faith in God and spirituality can also be important

mediators.[25] Sadly, religious leaders – who should represent compassion and healing – have often not only failed to listen and understand but sometimes contributed to the trauma and damage done, although the various religious institutions are now beginning to listen and to accept some of the responsibilities they have for past cases of sexual abuse.

In spite of the disillusionment of many with the behaviour of their church, some adult victims have a deep spirituality which acts as a strong aid to recovery. For them the capacity to forgive their abuser allows them to free themselves from the control of the past. Anger and lack of forgiveness can keep the adult victim locked in a destructive relationship with her abuser and allow the abuser to continue to ruin their lives. Forgiving does not mean excusing, but it allows the adult to let go of her own crippling anger and resentment and desire to punish her abuser. A rich spiritual life can give adult victims the strength to bear the pain of what has been done to them and to rebuild their lives.

Many adult victims of abuse also benefit from counselling, particularly counselling which views the sexual abuse within the context of other childhood, adolescent and adult difficulties. There is a huge variety of effects which result from sexual abuse. However, it is also important to realise that adult victims of sexual abuse have many symptoms which are experienced by victims of other kinds of serious child abuse. David Finkelhor cautions that 'sexual abuse is not necessarily the key which unlocks everything else',[26] good advice for both adult victims and counsellors.

Adult victims also need to know when they should go for help. One practitioner has listed four indicators to be on the alert for:[27]

1   intense anxiety, either generalised or focused (phobias, obsessions, et cetera)
2   depression or anxiety of crippling intensity – preventing the person from coping with normal life
3   any of the above when coupled with physical symptoms

4   feelings of unreality, of losing a grip on reality

Three critical times in the lives of many victims have also been identified as the most likely points at which counselling might be needed. These are:

1   immediately after the abuse event
2   at the time of marriage
3   at the time when their own children near the age at which their own abuse occurred

The long-term result of good counselling is that the child sexual abuse is put in place: it happened; it is over; it is healed; it ceases to be a central (even though hidden) focus. When a person can relate comfortably to the present rather than be dominated by the past, when she no longer feels like a victim but can grow and expand as a normal human being and get on with life, she has succeeded in leaving behind the crippling effects of her past abuse.

On the one hand, therefore, we need to recognise the fact that sexual abuse results in a wide variety of problems for victims, including damage to sexual development, the ability to trust, self-esteem, body image and so on. On the other hand, we need to recognise that the strong advocacy mentality of the past decade has led to an emphasis on the glass being half-empty rather than being half-full. For example, while adults with a history of sexual abuse have a three times greater risk of being depressed, 85 per cent of those with a history of sexual abuse are not currently depressed. Adult victims also have a fourteen times greater risk of being phobic but 93 per cent have no current phobia.[28]

A balanced perspective on the long-term impact of sexual abuse is important in order to inspire adult victims rather than discourage them. We need to focus more on the mediating life experiences which intervene and make the difference between adult victims coping and not coping.

Finally, we need to question the usefulness of adult victims of sexual abuse being labelled as survivors. In her book *Women Who*

Run with the Wolves,[29] Clarissa Pinkola Estes has the following to say to adults who label themselves as being survivors from adversities:

> Being able to say that one is a survivor is an accomplishment. For many, the power is in the name itself. And yet there comes a time in the individuation process when the threat or trauma is significantly past. Then is the time to go to the next stage after survivorship, to healing and thriving . . . Once the threat is past, there is a potential trap in calling ourselves by names taken on during the most terrible time of our lives. It creates a mind-set that is potentially limiting. It is not good to base the soul identity purely on the feats and losses and victories of the bad times . . . When a woman insists 'I am a survivor' over and over again once the time for its usefulness is past, the work ahead is clear. We must loosen the person's clutch on the survivor archetype. Otherwise nothing else can grow. I liken it to a tough little plant that managed – without water, sunlight, nutrients – to send out a brave and ornery little leaf anyway. In spite of it all . . . But thriving means, now that the bad times are behind, to put ourselves into occasions of the lush, the nutritive, the light, and there to flourish, to thrive with bushy, shaggy, heavy blossoms and leaves. It is better to name ourselves names that challenge us to grow as free creatures. That is thriving.

This is a wise passage which should be heeded not just by adult victims of abuse but by those who work with them, by the media who reinforce the 'forever victim' stereotype, and by the researchers who – rather than focusing on single cause and effect studies – need to take a broader perspective and focus also on the mediators which influence the adult victim's capacity to cope and which ultimately aid recovery.

9

A responsible approach to lessening child sexual abuse in our society

The dominant view of sexual abuse is that all responsibility for the abuse lies with the abuser. We, as non-abusing members of society, have no responsibility whatsoever for the fact that the abuse occurs. From time to time, we acknowledge that the abuser may himself have been a victim of abuse in childhood but this is not our fault. We are certainly not to blame for the increasingly public outpouring of cases of sexual and physical abuse that confront us – often daily – as we scan our newspapers or listen to the news on television or radio.

The questions I raise in this chapter challenge this dominant view. I believe that we as parents, educators, lawmakers or simply socially interacting human beings have some responsibility for the abuse that occurs in our midst. That responsibility presents itself in many guises from the everyday manner in which we relate to our children to the messages we allow society to convey on our behalf.

Let me first approach the issues around how we deal with our children in this climate of widespread revelations of sexual and physical abuse.

On a very basic level, we aim to teach our children to understand that they must say no to approaches of a sexual nature. But how are we passing on this message when often, in practice, we do not talk openly and honestly to children about their sexuality? How are children supposed to know what is and what is not a sexual approach? How can they tell the difference between intimate physical contact that is purely affectionate and intimate physical contact that has a sexual dimension? Do we, as adults, train them to differentiate?

Childhood sexuality is a complex subject that has not always been given the attention it deserves. So uncomfortable are many adults with their own sexuality that even to consider how children can and should express their sexuality is beyond them. This is a very unfortunate situation. Not only does it discourage children from expressing their sexuality but it leaves them very confused regarding what is and is not appropriate behaviour.

Psychologists now acknowledge that children can enjoy the intimacy and affection that often accompanies physical contact of a sexual nature.[1] They relish the special attention and sense of sharing a secret with an older person that so often is part of the scenario built up by an abusing adult (or teenager). Children may also feel physiologically aroused – albeit in an immature way – by the encounter.

Simply telling children to say no when they are touched on parts of their bodies covered by their swimming togs (as recommended in the current Stay Safe programme recently introduced into primary schools in the Republic of Ireland as a preventative measure against sex abuse) does not deal with the complex and sometimes conflicting feelings children can have in such situations. The resistance of some parents to such abuse prevention programmes and to the introduction of relationships and sexuality education also reflects a reluctance to acknowledge the role of sexuality in the lives of all individuals. Protestations about the need to 'protect children's innocence' can be better interpreted as a desire to keep children in ignorance, which is surely a form of abuse in itself.

Instead, we must, as mature human beings, teach them in an everyday way how to respond to varying levels of intimacy – from those familiar figures in their life and/or from strangers. This can be done only by nurturing a healthy approach to sexuality from an early age. The first thing adults must acknowledge is that children are sexual beings from the moment of birth.

Children learn about their bodies through the responses they get from curious exploration. Parents or guardians must learn to give positive responses to such exploration while at the same time explaining how some parts of their bodies, i.e. their willies or vaginas (unfortunately, there is no child-friendly word for the female sexual organ), are private. Only in this way can children learn that no one has the right to touch these parts of their bodies.

Giving age-appropriate answers to questions from children about their bodies and your own body lays the basis for the development of a positive and self-respecting body image. Together with the knowledge of the physical privacy they must preserve until they are older, this approach leaves children less vulnerable to sexual abuse. Through open and honest communication with their children, adults will develop a more mature understanding of their own sexuality. Conversely, by withdrawing from or entirely avoiding conversations of this nature, adults prevent children from learning what feels right (e.g. playful fun in the bath between parent and child) and what feels wrong (e.g. playful fun in the bath which focuses on the child's private parts). Such adults may themselves also continue to feel inhibited about their own sexuality.

Masturbation is another area of human sexuality around which numerous myths and half-truths have grown, many of them passed down to us in a society which condemned masturbation. Not so long ago in this country, it was even deemed to be a cause of mental illness. Masturbation is, however, a natural and some would say satisfying form of sexual gratification. Children will, in the course of the exploration of their bodies, occasionally masturbate. It is only when an adult tells them it is wrong that they will become confused and perhaps masturbate in a covert manner. While it is important to teach children that masturbation in public is highly inappropriate, discouraging them from doing so in private may prove counter-productive. As in other areas of developing sexual awareness, a family environment with many taboo subjects results in confusion and when children are confused, they are less likely to develop a strong sense of self-protection against potential abusive situations.

While the family is obviously the first and primary sphere of influence for children, the wider world of school, television and increasingly the Internet is a powerful source of information and commentary from which children glean all sorts of facts and fictions about life. Parents have a responsibility here to be the protectors of their children insomuch as they have some knowledge of what children are experiencing in these arenas.

Parents also need to monitor the contents of so-called 'teen' magazines which are often read by much younger children.[2] These magazines exploit young people's curiosity about sex and often contain sexually explicit material. Some readers may remember the outrage caused by a 'problem page' response which advised a ten-year-old to 'lie back and enjoy'. Apart from their obvious sexual messages, such magazines present young people with the overpowering message that to be successful (i.e. sexually attractive), they must be unhealthily thin, wear particular clothes and use particular make-up. On a broader level, we as adults need to question more the cultural fascination with beauty, weight, youth.

We must also realise that we have some responsibility for what is reflected to children from our contemporary society. By actively participating in and commenting (or not commenting) on the society we live in, we are ourselves either colluding with a society which tolerates abuse or seeking to live in one which discourages abusive relationships on all levels. We need to be less complacent about the media messages which exploit and objectify sexuality. We ignore at our peril the lack of control on videos available to young people which glorify abusive and coercive sexuality. In the light of evidence that exposure to such videos is one factor found to be significant in the lives of young adolescent males who sexually abuse children, a stronger adult monitoring of what is available to young people is clearly necessary.[3]

Abuse cannot simply be divided into indictable sexual or physical categories. Instead, it is an attitude or approach to people which we are all guilty of and victim to from time to time. And children are more prone to this approach than adults because often they have not yet learned how to protect themselves from such behaviour and neither have they learned the wrongfulness of it.

What I am really saying here is that there is a continuum of abuse in society, much of which is openly tolerated and sometimes condoned. This acceptance of the milder forms of abuse can, in turn, open the sluice-gates for the more deviant and punishable types of abuse to occur.

Take, for example, the widespread acceptance of the use of physical punishment on children. According to a recent survey, 76 per cent of adults feel that slapping a child with an open hand remains an acceptable form of punishment, and 16 per cent believe the same of slapping a child with a stick, cane or wooden spoon.[4] Developing alternative forms of discipline to physical punishment (such as withdrawing rewards like promised toys or days out) is one way of discontinuing this form of abuse of power over children by adults. The possibility of the corporal punishment of children by their parents becoming illegal is increasing all the time. The 1998 ruling by the European Court in favour of the English boy who claimed that his father's corporal punishment of him was unlawful is significant as a further step towards this.

Another more insidious example that comes to mind is how

little girls are transformed into grotesque Barbie-like miniature adults in the child beauty queen business in the United States. We may feel complacent that such abuse of children to meet some warped adult notion of entertainment could happen only in the material grossness of America, yet little girls in this country are taken to sunbeds to achieve an even tan before they participate in the spectacle that is their First Holy Communion.

The cynical exploitation of the pre-teen market through pop bands like the Spice Girls brings into question how ambivalent we really are about the early sexualisation (in an adult manner) of our children. Here, often in the absence of any other sex education, pre-teenage girls are encouraged to dress seductively, dance erotically and generally act out sexual fantasies which are much too complex for their personal stage of development.

While we can individually change our punishment methods (e.g. giving rewards for good behaviour instead of slapping children for bad behaviour) and encourage others to do likewise, we cannot censor the pop phenomenon which engrosses children's attention. However, assertive, well-placed adult comments about pop music videos, television dramas and so on do help children to understand these dominant messages in the context of their own lives.

As voters, we also have a say in what is done to prevent child abuse at the widest levels of legislation and government policy. While the introduction of the Child Care Act 1991 in the Republic of Ireland was widely welcomed, the 1998 United Nations Committee (which monitored the implementation of the 1989 Convention on the Rights of the Child – ratified by Ireland in 1992) highlighted that much more was needed in Ireland to fulfil all the aspirations of the Convention.

Voluntary organisations such as Barnardo's show how the needs of many Irish children are far from being met in the areas of protection and care, health, welfare, education and their right to freedom of expression and access to information.[5] It is unacceptable that Ireland still does not have a comprehensive national strategy for children. This leaves policy vulnerable to ad hoc decisions made by the three separate departments of health, justice and education.

Preventative measures need to be given priority rather than the current policy of reacting to crises in the area of child protection. There is a great need to combat child and family poverty and to put resources into education, early child development programmes and measures to combat early school leaving. And although the United Nations, the European Union and national governments all have a role to play in increasing the protection of children, we need to resist the temptation to believe that we can prevent the abuse and exploitation of children through legislation alone. Measures such as mandatory reporting of sex abuse and sex offenders registers are quick-fix solutions which give the impression that something is being done.

It is only through all the above steps that we can create an environment in which sexual abuse is less likely to occur and our children are better equipped to remove themselves from situations when they recognise the first signs of abuse. Protecting children from abuse is an individual and community responsibility. So too is ensuring that children are protected from the deviant developmental experiences and adverse home, community and cultural conditions which result in so many young people now starting to engage in sexually abusive behaviours against others at an early age.

10

A cure for sex offending?
Why treatment not punishment
is the best approach

The publicity given to high-profile cases of child sex abuse has led to an emotional knee-jerk reaction by the public and an inability to see beyond the imprisonment of the offender as the only way to deal with sexual abusers. An 'out of sight, out of mind' attitude prevails. No account is taken of the fact that punishment on its own is pointless and that it does not prevent abusers from reoffending. Even less account is taken of the fact that most sex offenders will remain in prison for only a few years and that few avail of the limited treatment on offer there. There is just one treatment programme, which can cater for only 10 men each year, available to the 280 sex offenders currently in Irish prisons. Even within this limited service, in the absence of treatment being mandatory, those most in need of treatment are least likely to avail of it.

The vast majority of sex offenders who do receive prison sentences (and it must be noted that only a tiny minority of sex offenders end up in prison)[1] will slip back into the community and research indicates that without treatment, the chances of them re-offending are very high. Some research shows that 35 per cent of sex offenders who go untreated reoffend and that treatment reduces this rate to 8.5 per cent.

The average sex offender in prison associates only with other sex offenders as he is segregated from the so-called ordinary decent criminals. He will not receive any confrontational education about his responsibility for the abusive behaviour. His excuses, twisted thinking and psychological projections will not be challenged. His relatives outside the prison may also feel sorry for him. All of this combines to make the sex offender feel that he is the injured party. He will feel self-righteous and hard-done-by and blame the police, the social workers, the child for telling, his wife for not having sex with him – anyone but himself.

By the time he is released, he is likely to have a huge chip on his shoulder and if his psychological distortions and denials of abuse have not been challenged, he is likely to reoffend. This time, he will have learned from his mistakes (which resulted in him being found out) so more children are at risk of being deprived of their right to a childhood free from the violation of sexual abuse.

I believe that mandatory treatment for those few offenders who do end up in prison would offer immediate benefit. However, if we are really serious about our stated concern to prevent child abuse, a comprehensive approach to the problems must replace mere punishment. This approach needs to include the provision of alternatives to custodial sentences for some low-risk sex offenders whose suitability would be decided on following an assessment of each offender (the degree of danger he represents, and his openness to remorse and rehabilitation). There is also a need to address the common perception that all abusers are alike and to accept that they vary in their insight, remorsefulness and levels of manipulation and dangerousness. (See chapter 5.)

Society, backed up by the law and the media, finds it very difficult to view victims and offenders as anything other than separate, distinct and antagonistic groups of individuals. The fact that, for many victims, the imprisonment of the abuser, especially if he is a family member, is not helpful, is often not acknowledged publicly. The victim's affections for the individual, sometimes their guilt feelings for their own perceived participation in the abuse, and pressure from other family members can leave her with a greater sense of guilt and a strong sense of alienation from the family. (See chapter 3.)

Many adults who were abused as children do not want to see the person who abused them imprisoned. Often, their main concern is that he should receive treatment in order to prevent other children from being abused. I believe that both children who are currently being abused (particularly older children) and adults who were abused in the past are more likely to come forward and disclose their abuse if a well-publicised alternative to the present adversarial legal process existed.

The legal system is far from victim-friendly although some efforts are now being made to address this.[2] Offenders are often advised by their solicitors to plead not guilty and this advice leaves the victim, who is merely a witness in the case, to establish guilt in spite of her confusion, guilt and pain. The resulting court case results in an unwanted and unhelpful high profile. An inquisitorial legal process (as used in countries such as France) would be much less traumatic for the victim. In such a system, focus is placed on establishing the facts and then providing whatever evidence is necessary (the offender has to prove his innocence rather than the victim having to prove her guilt). Counselling is also necessary for both the victim and her family and for the other forgotten innocent victims – the offender's family.

Child sexual abuse is a crime that must not be condoned and the abuser must always be held responsible for his actions. If he is dangerous and uncooperative, a custodial sentence may be the only option. However, if we really care for the victim, we need to provide a comprehensive service which caters for victims, offenders and the families of both. The provision of a community-based treatment for the offender should, in my view, form an integral part of that service. I believe that when the offender remains in the community to obtain treatment, this offers him a much more effective way to take responsibility for his actions. In prison, the offender does not have to deal with the everyday response of his family and the community to his crime. Even if he does opt for treatment, it occurs in an artificial child-free world.[3] The offender who continues to live in his community (albeit with built-in safeguards which include receiving treatment and supervision by the probation and welfare service) has to be seen to change.

It is very easy, when we hear about cases of sexual abuse, to respond using the same techniques of denial and twisted thinking which we condemn in the offender. All too often, we, as a society, adhere to a model of control and punishment. We have a particular position to uphold and defend and our defence mechanisms may not be any less suspect than those of the abuser. It is very easy to adopt a role of defender/protector of children without questioning our own motivation and the largely un-conscious forces that may be influencing us in circumstances which are both complex and emotive.

We need to put aside our personal revulsion with regard to child sexual abuse and look at the abuser as a fellow human being. We need to enter into his world and listen to him in the same way that we listen to victims. We need to judge the actions of abusers on a case-by-case basis. Listening to what sex offenders have to say does not mean that we allow ourselves to be con-trolled or manipulated by them any more than listening to an alcoholic will necessarily lead to a complete surrender of our abil-ity to distinguish fact from fiction.

Community-based treatment is not a soft option but rather a more efficient and cost-effective approach to the prevention of child sexual abuse. Prison is just society's way of avenging itself on the abuser. Unpalatable as it may be, the treatment of sex offenders needs to be an integral part of any child protection services. A realistic compromise needs to be contemplated which balances the risk of further abuse against minimising the trauma and confusion of the victim and other family members. In the event of any conflict between the victim's rights and those of the abuser, the victim's rights should always take precedence.

The current community-based treatment programme run by the North-Western Health Board is not an alternative to custodial sentencing, nor is its purpose to prevent sex offenders from going to prison. It is rather a response to the reality that, without treatment, sex offenders are not going to magically change, and with punishment alone, they remain a threat to children. Through our work, we have come to believe that it is unlikely that the majority of sex offenders will ever confess and seek help on their own initiative. The typical sex offender is not adequately aware of the effects of his abuse. He therefore refuses to accept that he has done anything wrong and sees no need to reform. When his abusive actions are revealed, his main objective becomes dealing with the crisis. This he usually attempts to do with promises, threats and deals of some kind. It is important to recognise that, for many offenders, once the crisis is over, these promises are no longer relevant and do not imply any significant change of behaviour or any firm purpose of amendment.

Members of our treatment team who have years of experience in dealing with clients who abuse alcohol recognise a lot of parallels in the behaviour of the sex offender and that of the alcoholic. These parallels are particularly noteworthy in both groups' denial and persistent refusal to look at the effects of the abuse on other people. In the past (and even still today by some professionals), alcoholics were regarded as hopeless cases who could not benefit from treatment because of their lack of insight and motivation to recover. Now alcoholics are deemed a suitable treatment group and various alcohol programmes exist throughout the world with varying levels of success. We would hope that, at some time in the future, the assessment and treatment of sex offenders would be considered as much a necessary and everyday service as the treatment of alcoholics now is.

Meanwhile, those working with sex offenders are, to some extent, stigmatised by association and the work being done is afforded scant credibility and little funding. However, the treatment of those sex offenders who are 'treatable' is an essential component in reducing unacceptable child abuse. While it is agreed that like alcohol addiction, there is no permanent cure for sex offending, many offenders can achieve control over their behaviour and cease to abuse.

The men who attend our community-based treatment programme are referred to us by social workers, the police or solicitors or come on their own initiative (usually as a result of family pressure). What all of these men have in common is that their sexual abuse of children has been discovered by others. No offender has yet disclosed his own abuse of a child and then sought treatment. However, we are encouraged by the slow trickle of men who are coming forward to seek help for a sexual attraction towards children upon which they have not acted but are fearful of so doing. These men have usually experienced sexual abuse themselves. It is hoped that the provision of treatment will increasingly encourage the attendance of such men – those who have not yet offended but who believe that they have the potential to engage in sexually abusive behaviour.

The clients who attend the group treatment are those who have already sexually abused children. At present, we accept all offenders who are motivated to attend regardless of whether they are facing or have faced the legal consequences of their actions. This differs from policy in other countries where sex offenders are accepted for treatment only after their cases have been processed by the courts. As the purpose of providing treatment for offenders is to reduce reoffending, we feel that this criterion is not feasible within the Irish context. Firstly, the number of cases where legal proceedings are taken against the abuser represents only a fraction of all sex abuse. Secondly, even when legal proceedings are taken against the abuser, there are long delays between the reporting of the crime and a decision being made as to whether there will be a prosecution, and between the decision to prosecute and the court appearance. For these reasons and in the interests of child protection, we spread our net widely.

Our only prerequisite for attending the treatment programme is that the men admit that they have committed a crime and are prepared to take responsibility for their behaviour. This usually means making a statement to the police, acknowledging their guilt. The men who attend treatment therefore include those who have no criminal charges proffered against them, those who are awaiting a decision by the Director of Public Prosecutions as to whether charges will be brought against them, those who are awaiting court appearances, those who have had their sentences adjourned to enable them to attend treatment under the supervision of the probation and welfare service, and those who have completed prison sentences.

While in practice we accept this diverse group, we would see value in the idea of mandatory treatment. The optimum circumstances for motivating an offender to engage in treatment are where a suspended prison sentence is combined with supervision. In one case, an offender with a suspended prison sentence who was not engaging fully in treatment was reported back to the court. The judge then imposed a five-week prison sentence in order to show him what his options were. This resulted in a dramatic improvement in his participation in the group.

Over the past twelve years of running the programme, we have seen many of the men confront the reality of their sexually abusive behaviour and the damage they have done to children. Only 3 per cent have – to the best of our knowledge – reoffended.

The majority of the men attending the programme do so on a voluntary basis. They are free to leave at any time and a small number have found the treatment approach so challenging that they decided to do so and 'take their chances' with the court system. The attendance of sex offenders in treatment is often viewed with suspicion, their motivation regarded as being an attempt to avoid a custodial sentence.[4] Yet there is evidence to suggest that the majority of successful programmes are those conducted with offenders who are mandated to attend or who are enticed by the promise of a reduction in supervision. The ideal situation therefore is to have leverage to encourage participation but intrinsically motivated offenders can also benefit from treatment. This is the case for the men who continue to attend our programme, even when there are no legal sanctions compelling them to do so.

We have found attendance levels to be very good, all the more so when you take into consideration that many of the men travel considerable distances to the treatment centre.

Once the initial work of engagingÅ and motivating the men has been done, we have been impressed by their levels of openness and honesty, and their willingness to divulge information about previously unknown incidents of abuse which they have committed or to report incidents in which they felt they had been at risk of abusing again, knowing that the reporting of such information may, in some cases, influence the content of reports prepared by the treatment team. We believe that we are significantly reducing the risk of reoffending. Many sex offenders have emerged from treatment with insight and a level of personal development which makes them not only safer to children but more complete human beings who will, it is hoped, contribute to society rather than take from it.[5]

An additional benefit of a community-based treatment programme for sex offenders is that it enables professionals to work with both victims and offenders at the same time. Contrary to some schools of thought which question the effectiveness of this, we have gained great insights which have been beneficial to both groups. Our work with offenders has enabled us to help victims understand the subtlety of the techniques used by abusers which leave victims feeling guilty and responsible. Meanwhile, we bring to the offenders a real rather than a textbook understanding of the effects of their behaviour on victims. This allows us to challenge their distortions which, in turn, helps them gain that essential empathy with their victims that will ultimately prevent them from reoffending. Overall, our work with both groups has given us an increased awareness of the complexities of abusive relationships and the vulnerability of victims in the unequal balance of power which is the hallmark of such relationships.

Conclusion

The way forward

This book is written at the end of a decade in Irish society in which the belief by good people that the world is a safe and secure place has been eroded. Shock has been heaped upon shock, and grief upon grief, as more and more revelations emerged about the violation of the most vulnerable members of our community by those once presumed to care for and protect them.

The existence of incest as a perversion of the sacredness of the family in Irish life was the first harsh reality to be faced. Efforts were made to understand it as a regrettable leftover of a traditional patriarchal system in which fathers dominated their families and had the power to make sexual use of their children. However, this explanation was challenged by the ensuing evidence that vulnerable children who had been placed in the care of the state had been abused not by their fathers but by those employed to protect them. Adults with whom responsible, caring parents had implicitly trusted their children (swimming coaches, scout/youth leaders, teachers) were the next to be exposed as wolves in sheep's clothing. The final betrayal of trust was the revelation of abuse by priests, so revered in this society.

Perhaps the greatest myth of all is now being shattered with the stories of the brutal physical abuse of children by nuns in the recent past, followed by the current evidence that women also sexually abuse children. It is not surprising therefore that so many have responded to this bombardment of the unthinkable with denial, confusion or a sense of helplessness.

Still, I see a way forward in my belief that Irish society has not yet fully embraced the age of individualism which involves the much-lamented death of the community, in which the resolve of ordinary people to keep to themselves allows evil to flourish. Moral outrage is needed in order to change the world, but the intense longing for revenge which child abuse provokes needs to be tempered by responsible people with greater insights into the consequences of acting out this longing. We have to be honest with ourselves about the capacity in all of us to do terrible things and how it is in our most intimate relationships that we can be most abusive. For all of us, sex offenders represent the darkest side of ourselves which we cannot bear to shed light on, and in our scapegoating and demonising of them, we can feel more complacent about our own righteousness.

True preventative work involves us all bearing some responsibility for the attitudes towards children and the society which we have created, out of which abuses occur. This does not absolve the individual from taking the responsibility for the crime which he/she has committed and society is also right to demand that a price is exacted from those who violate children. Punishment should not, however, preclude rehabilitation, and we must heed all the evidence available that treatment greatly reduces the risks of sexual reoffending. The advocacy of treatment for all identified sex offenders is not a bleeding heart do-gooder's response but rather a commonsense one. But this is still an end-of-the-line response and there is an abundance of research which points us to the ways in which we can prevent abuse.

The earliest intervention is, of course, before birth, where we need better policy in perinatal care and parent care. We have collective responsibility for creating an environment in the home, community and culture for all children which is nurturing, non-abusive and sexually healthy. We also have collective culpability for the lack of any national strategy in relation to childcare in Ireland which would help to achieve this with combined policy in the areas of health, justice and education. At present, these three separate departments each deal with different aspects of childcare, and while the Department of Health has had 'and Children' added to its title, there is little evidence that this has improved co-ordination of services. There has, however, been significant progress in the area with the implementation of the Child Care Act 1991, the purpose of which was to update the law in relation to the care of children, particularly children who have been assaulted, ill-treated, neglected or sexually abused or who are at risk of any of the above.

Nevertheless, there is a need to be wary of emotive ad hoc legislation which, in the absence of any national strategy, is introduced as a political response to perceived crises. Any measures which claim to tackle abuse have to be judged according to the outcomes which they produce for children. Mandatory reporting and sex offender registers are examples of quick-fix solutions which sound good but achieve little.

More realistic ways forward involve implementing known preventative measures which will benefit all of society. The re-educating and training of all of those juvenile and adult offenders currently identified in order to prevent further victims is a logical first step. This involves a comprehensive approach which recognises that low-risk offenders can often be better rehabilitated in the community than in prison. The option of sentences being suspended, conditional upon the offender taking part in a treatment programme while being monitored, is a sensible one, which also acknowledges the evidence that the most successful treatment work is done with sex offenders on a mandated basis.[1]

For those offenders not assessed as suitable for community treatment, mandatory treatment in prison is necessary.[2] There is a lot of value in the case made for indeterminate sentences to ensure that sex offenders are returned to society only when their risk of reoffending is deemed to be significantly reduced. Even then, release should be conditional on supervision and follow-up treatment in the community. Progressive legislation has already been introduced in Northern Ireland (Criminal Justice [NI] Order 1996) which allows sex offenders who are considered suitable to be supervised in the community for the final quarter of their sentence. The fact that a minority of offenders are not amenable to treatment also needs to be responded to in a way that protects children. Indeterminate sentences would reassure the public that they are being protected from these dangerous individuals (or at least from those in this category who reach the courts).

Other commonsense preventative measures include the use of educational programmes in schools such as the current Stay Safe programme in Irish primary schools[3] and the planned relationship and sexuality education module at both primary and secondary level.[4] The media also have a lot of power to influence the attitudes of the general public. In the past decade, journalists have done invaluable work in increasing public awareness of the existence of sexual abuse. Through media coverage, many victims realised that they were not alone, they were able to overcome their shame and guilt and go on to tell the painful stories of their childhood. Unfortunately, sexual abuse is no longer news except for the most extreme cases and it sometimes appears as if the media's treatment of child sexual abuse has become a contest in sensationalism. The reporting of minute details of sexual abuse cases leaves the media accused of social pornography and places victims at the receiving end of another injustice.[5]

While a greater awareness of child sexual abuse is to be welcomed, in some cases the pendulum has swung too far and the task of achieving true engagement with the problem has been set back by overzealous professionals. The public have had to accept that professionals can and do make mistakes in opinion, judgement and practice.

The Royal College of Psychiatrists in London, which governs psychiatrists in Ireland and Britain, recently came out strongly against sex abuse being diagnosed on the basis of 'regressed memories' and 'false memory syndrome'. These cases centred on vulnerable and suggestive adults being persuaded by therapists that they had been sexually abused as children.

There is also evidence that in the past, due to a misplaced emphasis on sexual abuse as the cause of all childhood symptoms and in the absence of adequate procedures, some professionals pressurised children into making allegations that they had been sexually abused. As a result of this, families have been ruined and there has been great personal anguish and suffering for those falsely accused. There is the fear that publicity given to false accusations will have a negative impact on public and professional attitudes towards the victim of sexual abuse, making it harder to persuade victims to come forward and to achieve the protection of children.

These fears should be offset against what has been achieved. Public awareness of child sexual abuse has been raised very successfully over a short period of time. More accepting public attitudes have encouraged adults who were sexually abused as children to come forward and receive help. It is now hoped that children will also benefit from this, and that, combined with preventative educational programmes in schools, it will make them less likely to be manipulated by their abusers into keeping silent. The view that there is no hope of moral progress or atonement in those who commit such crimes has been disproved with increasing evidence of the success of treatment programmes. It remains for each of us to challenge the utterly bleak view that the abuse of children is something that we have no responsibility for and can do nothing about.

We must end with the image of the glass as half-full rather than half-empty, and take with us the conviction that we can make the world a truly safer place for all our children.

Appendix
What happens behind closed doors: the community-based treatment programme in practice

Since 1986, a multidisciplinary, multi-agency team, with person-nel from the North-Western Health Board and the Department of Justice, has been providing a community-based treatment programme for male sex offenders in Letterkenny, County Donegal. This programme was the first of its kind in the Republic of Ireland.

Even twelve years on, assessment/treatment resources for adult sex offenders remain very scarce. Work being done in the area is mainly confined to Dublin and includes programmes in Arbour Hill Prison and the Granada Institute. There is, however, an encouraging increase in the provision of treatment pro-grammes for juvenile sex offenders.

In the mid-1980s in the north-west of Ireland, as elsewhere in the country, there was a dramatic increase in the number of referrals to the Health Board services relating to the sexual abuse of children – from 9 in 1984 to a peak of 150 in 1987.[1] The probation service also subsequently found itself involved with an increasing number of sex offenders. The rise in referrals was mainly seen as a consequence of the work of the Women's Movement in increasing public awareness of the sexual abuse of children. Professionals in the health ser-vices had to rapidly acquire additional skills and training to enable them to deal with the increase in their workload in this demanding area. Nationally, the emphasis was, and to a large extent continues to be, on the need to rescue children from the trauma of sexual abuse, which was also the focus of the media publicity. The Department of Health funded two specialist units for the assessment of suspected cases of child sexual abuse in response to the increase of referrals in the 1980s. These units catered only for the victims of

abuse and there were no equivalent services set up for offenders. A story is told which best sums up the official response to
the increase in referrals of children who had been sexually
assaulted:

> Once upon a time, there was a small village on the edge of a
> river. The people there were good and life in the village was
> good. One day a villager noticed a baby floating down the
> river. The villager promptly jumped into the river and swam
> out to save the baby from drowning. The next day the same
> villager was walking along the river bank and noticed two
> babies in the river. He called for help and both babies were res-
> cued from the swift waters. And the next day, four babies were
> seen caught in the turbulent current. And then eight, then
> more, and still more. The villagers organised themselves
> quickly, setting up watch towers and training teams of swim-
> mers who could resist the swift waters and rescue babies. Res-
> cue squads were soon working twenty-four hours a day. Each
> day the number of helpless babies floating down the river in-
> creased. While not all the babies, now very numerous, could
> be saved, the villagers felt that they were doing very well to
> save as many as they could each day. Indeed the village priest
> blessed them in their good work. And life in the village con-
> tinued on that basis. One day, however, someone raised the
> question *'But where are all these babies coming from? Who is throw-
> ing them into the river? Why? Let's organise a team to go upstream and
> see who's doing it.'* The seeming logic of the elders countered:
> *'And if we go upstream, who will operate the rescue operation? We
> need every concerned person here.'* *'But don't you see,'* cried one lone
> voice, *'if we find out who is throwing them in, we can stop the problem
> and no babies will drown? By going upstream we can eliminate the cause
> of the problem.'* *'It's too risky.'* And so the numbers of babies in
> the river increased daily. Those saved increased, but those who
> drown increase even more.[2]

In the far-flung and isolated region of Donegal in the mid-
1980s, during informal conversations over cups of coffee, professionals began to question the need to 'go upstream' and tackle the
source of this increasing flow of human trauma. The first group

treatment programme for sex offenders in Ireland originated
from these casual meetings.

The treatment team which came together includes a
consultant psychiatrist, a psychiatric social worker, a behavioural
psychotherapist and a senior clinical psychologist from the health
service, and two probation and welfare officers from the Department of Justice. Each professional brought to the team his/her
own particular perspective and expertise.

Our first task was to obtain the, at that time, very scarce information about sex offenders and treatment approaches. A holiday
trip to the United States by the then senior psychologist yielded
valuable information gathered from established treatment
centres visited there. The work of Ray Wyre and his team in
the pioneering Gracewell Clinic in England was added to this.[3]
Later a social worker on holiday in New Zealand brought back
information on the Kia Marama programme being run in
Rolleston Prison.[4] In all of the diverse information which we
gathered, we found many common approaches.

Over the past twelve years, we have integrated strands from
many different sources. We have modified and adapted them to
make them our own in order to suit our particular circumstances
and client group.

Information about sex offenders and treatment methods has
improved greatly in this time. There are now numerous publications covering treatment approaches and workbooks for offenders to assist in reinforcing treatment aims. All treatment
programmes for sex offenders have similar content. A usual format consists of three stages covering assessment, intervention and
relapse prevention. There is overlap between these stages and
there is ongoing assessment and evaluation. The time allocated
to the treatment process varies depending on resources available.

Our programme is a 'rolling' one requiring the men (following assessment) to attend group treatment for one full day each
week for six consecutive weeks. In the breaks between each six-
week 'run', some of the men attend for individual sessions, new
referrals are seen for assessment and 'after-care' days are held for

those no longer attending on an ongoing basis. There is no set time limit within which an offender will complete treatment. This can vary from one to several years, depending on the strength of the individual's defences and his intellectual ability.

Our focus remains firmly fixed on reducing the rate of re-offending by child sex offenders. With this in mind, the function of the initial assessment is to obtain information to determine the suitability of the offender for a community-based programme, and if he is suitable, what his treatment needs are. The format of the assessment procedures may vary in different programmes but usually involves individual sessions initially with the offender.

In our programme, the men who have been referred are first interviewed over a number of sessions by two team members. We have an equal number of male and female therapists in the team, which allows a consistent gender balance in both assess-ment and group work.

The initial assessment is carried out by the psychologist (fe-male) and the behavioural psychotherapist (male). In addition to the individual interviews, we also use the first six weeks of attendance in group as an integral part of the offender's assess-ment. It is only at this stage that a decision is made by the team as to whether the offender should be offered a place on the pro-gramme. Information gathered during assessment involves areas such as

- personal history, including sexual history
- self-image
- thinking patterns, positive or negative
- social competence, interpersonal relationships
- intellectual ability
- psychiatric health
- details of the abusive behaviour and the scale and pattern of his offending
- cognition, i.e. attitudes towards women, the harm abuse does to victims, sex with children, et cetera
- sexual attitudes and arousal patterns

- self-control
- safeguards in environment – family/social relationships, employment
- problem-solving ability

This information is gathered from a variety of sources, including structured interviews with the offender, psychometric tests, victim's report, offender's statement to the police, information from other professionals and family members.

During the assessment, abusers are challenged in a supportive way to acknowledge their most secret, hidden and shameful sexual behaviour. This is an extremely difficult thing to do. Each individual responds in a different way, but over the years, we have witnessed a lot of common responses. The initial presentation of the offender is usually that of a visibly shaken, nervous, often tearful individual who is reeling under the impact of his abuse having been disclosed. His life – as he has known it – may have collapsed. He may have lost his family, his self-esteem and his sense of personal safety. He may have had to leave his home and live elsewhere, often in inadequate accommodation. He may have lost his job. He will be experiencing the various reactions of his family and often the community, the mixture of shock, anger, outrage, hurt and disbelief.

For many offenders, being powerful and controlling has been their only way of relating to the world. The disclosure of the abuse reverses this and the offender experiences powerlessness. He will often attend for assessment in the hope that he will be able to regain the life he previously knew. He will sometimes be very insistent that he knows now that what he did was wrong and that he will never do it again. The logical conclusion of this belief for him is that he can apologise to the victim and resume his previous lifestyle. He will protest that he is really very glad that the abuse was discovered, it is 'a burden off his back'. He will become confused when asked why, if this is the case, he did not stop the abuse himself. He may be very angry, and eager to blame everyone except himself for his downfall. He will blame his wife for their poor relationship, his family, the social workers, the police, and his victim for telling. He will claim that he has come to get 'help', but that 'help' usually means taking away some of the unpleasant consequences of his behaviour for him. In addition to the minimising of his offences through the use of such phrases as 'it just happened' and 'I only', we often hear 'I can't remember'. The loss of memory is usually about abuse which occurred when the offender was drinking. Our response to this is to express concern that, if he has blackouts when drinking, he is potentially a very dangerous person. We suggest that it is possible he has committed even more serious crimes when drunk than those of which he is being accused. A remarkable degree of recall about the sexual abuse usually results.

Overall, we recognise the difficulties for the offender in accepting full responsibility for his abusive behaviour during initial assessment. As a minimum we will require him to acknowledge that he has committed a crime; making a statement to the police admitting his guilt usually covers this. His ability to see his offending as a problem, and his willingness to make the commitment to attend treatment are also necessary for the acceptance of the offender into the next stage of treatment. Treatment for alcohol or other substance abuse is another prerequisite and we liaise closely with the addiction treatment services. A small number of offenders opt out at the assessment stage.

The challenge for us as therapists is how to counterbalance the responses of denial and hiding which being shamed has provoked in those men who do attend treatment. We have found it useful first to acknowledge their reaction by asking them to write about it. From this work we get a sense of how one-dimensional they have become as a result of their sex offending being discovered. All other aspects of their lives are ignored.

> I have stopped going to town and the shops. I have stopped socialising. I am afraid to even answer the phone. All I want to do is hide away. I am just totally and utterly disgusted with myself.

People are nice to my face but what are they saying behind my back? 'Have you any kids? Keep them away from him. He would have their knickers off before long! He's a f—ing pervert!'

Everyone close to me is ashamed to have known and trusted me. I cannot face going into the canteen at work. Everyone avoids me.

I am afraid to go to visit my father in the hospital. You always meet people you know there.

I know people are calling me a dirty f—er and a right bastard. I would say the same myself if I heard someone was a child abuser.

The shame has made me feel useless. It takes away from the person I was. It makes me feel suicidal, especially when my abuse was in the local paper.

I would like to fade away and die. If I could turn back the clock of time I would do everything different but I can't. I have to live now with the clock of time going forward and not back.

The men are also asked to shift their focus to what are called 'alternative stories' about themselves from their past as well as stories they would like to be told about themselves in the future.[5] We acknowledge that, while work in the treatment programme focuses on their sexually abusive behaviour, we realise that there is more to their lives than that. We recognise that they also may be good husbands, sons, brothers, neighbours. They may be good providers, skilled workers and talented in many areas. The men identify what they regard as their good points.

I would be generous to the charities. I get a lump in my throat when I see things that go on in the world on TV. I had money saved to put in central heating but I gave it to charity. We still have no oil in.

I saved enough money to build an extension to the house. My wife is very proud of me for what I have done.

I do all the painting and decorating in the house and I have great pride in having the place clean and tidy.

I do painting and drawing with my children. We feed the birds in the mornings and I advise my children to be good to all animals and birds.

I am not money-driven and I often done days and days of work for neighbours and friends and I would not take any money.

My neighbours always know that they can get me, even in the middle of the night, if a cow is in trouble calving.

The exploration of all the positive aspects of the offender's life motivates him to move from hiding and blaming to working on ways in which he can start 'behaving above suspicion'. This is a step-by-step process that will begin a new lived moral order. The offender's full co-operation during treatment is part of this, as is his working on what he needs to do within his family and community to regain trust and demonstrate genuine remorse for his actions. This in turn involves a detailed examination of his behaviour before and when offending, and links up with his work on understanding the steps that led up to his abusive behaviour. The emphasis is on how 'actions speak louder than words'. This approach gives the offender something meaningful to work towards. A context is set in treatment of working together to protect children. The individual offender's capacity to become a caring, protective, non-abusing adult is acknowledged.

This is possibly the single most important aspect of the philosophical ethos underpinning the treatment of the men who sexually abuse children. The recognition of the whole person in treatment rather than acceptance of society's view of the one-dimensional monster is crucial. It motivates the offender to change his behaviour rather than to respond to the experience of being shamed in an angry, blaming way. Our priority is to protect children, and such a response increases the risk of further children being abused.

The intervention aspects of treatment programmes are geared towards achieving that critical change necessary to protect against further abuse. The underlying approach in most programmes is 'Cognitive, Behavioural and Psychotherapeutic', i.e. by addressing the thoughts, feelings and behaviour related to their offending, sex offenders can learn to control that behaviour. Behavioural techniques can be effective in controlling the deviant sexual fantasies which contributed to the abuse, but abusers have no reason to use them if they still believe their offending did no harm. The psychotherapeutic and cognitive restructuring aspects of the programmes address issues such as attitudes to women and children, power in relationships, and the self-image and previous lifestyle of the offender. It is now recognised that there are many causes for sex offending and the range of therapeutic approaches attempts to match these.

In our programme we use treatment goals adapted from American programmes as the basis for both group and individual treatment.[6] These goals are:

1 Each sex offender needs a complete, individualised assessment and treatment plan and continuous evaluation.
2 Each sex offender needs to
   (a) accept responsibility for the offences which he has committed and
   (b) have an understanding of the sequences of thoughts, feelings, events, circumstances and arousal stimuli that make up the 'offence syndrome' which precedes his involvement in sexually abusive behaviour.
3 Each sex offender needs to learn how to
   (a) intervene and break into his offence pattern at its very first sign and
   (b) call upon appropriate methods, tools or procedures he has learned in order to suppress, control, manage and stop the behaviour.
4 Each sex offender needs to engage in a re-education and re-socialisation process in order to
   (a) replace antisocial thoughts and behaviours with

       pro-social ones,

(b)   acquire a positive self-concept with new attitudes and expectations for himself and

(c)   learn new social and sexual skills to help cultivate positive, satisfying, pleasurable and non-threatening relationships with others.

5   Each sex offender needs

(a)   relapse prevention training and

(b)   continual post-programme access to therapeutic treatment so he can maintain permanently a safe lifestyle.

Goals 2 and 3 form the core of initial individual and group work. Two therapists, one male and one female, facilitate all groups. The goals are achieved through a combination of educational input about defence mechanisms and offending patterns and the men doing individual work both in the group and in the form of written homework exercises.

Goal 4 is a response to the awareness that the men need a lot more than the understanding and knowledge of their offending in order to prevent them from repeating it. In this goal we place a lot of emphasis on the men's development of victim awareness and empathising skills. This, as discussed earlier, is one of the most difficult goals to achieve.

Over the years, we have discovered that the usually recommended techniques of providing information about the impact of the abuse on victims are ineffective. The men's defences in this area are very strong. A full acceptance of the effects of their actions involves them first reconnecting with the feelings they themselves experienced when they were victimised as children. These feelings are connected with incidents of physical and emotional abuse as well as sexual. It is stressed that these early abuse experiences cannot be 'blamed' for his abuse of others, but the repressed feelings being re-experienced is the best route to empathy with the feelings of his victim.

Goal 4 includes:

- examining gender-role behaviour, and challenging their

stereotypical notions about the roles of women and men
- the provision of sex education in order to overcome the myths and misconceptions about human sexuality
- the referral on to a general social skills group of those offenders who have deficits in this area

Goal 5 involves teaching the men to cope with specific difficulties that may arise which may signal an increased risk of relapse. These difficulties will be a result of his awareness of his offence cycle from the work done to achieve goals 2 and 3. We have adapted from a New Zealand programme the warning signs that each individual offender has to be alert to.[7] These include 'seemingly irrelevant choices (SIC)', which are decisions and choices that in themselves appear innocuous or irrelevant to the possibility of reoffending but that lead to 'high-risk situations (HRS)', situations or circumstances that weaken or threaten a person's sense of control over his behaviour. These high-risk situations lead to the 'problem of immediate gratification (PIG)', which is the urge to have sexual pleasure or release.

The men are asked to identify what for them are 'lapses' – things they would do in the high-risk situations which make sexual abuse more likely to reoccur. They are also alerted to the danger of the 'what the hell' effect – thoughts and feelings during a lapse which make reoffending more likely. The thoughts are often to do with the offender's knowing that he has begun to break certain rules about not reoffending and his defiant response to this. Each offender has to be aware of what his 'offence precursor signals' are, which will indicate that he has lapsed and is secretly now building up to an actual offence. The signals are caused by the tension in the person who is caught between the desire to reoffend and the fear of the consequences.

In group treatment, these signals often express themselves as a certain grandiosity, a belief that they now understand all about their offending and should no longer have to attend, being critical, irritable and missing appointments.

Tom's seemingly irrelevant choices first involved him 'just

happening' to be frequently passing the local primary school at going-home time. He then 'just happened' to make his casual visits to his friends' house at about the time when their ten-year-old daughter, Claire, was doing her homework. Tom is particularly good with children and they take to him easily. Claire's parents were pleased when Tom showed an interest in her school work and started to help her with her homework. The progression to high-risk situation came with Tom bringing Claire on her own 'for a spin' into town to get her a comic as a reward for doing her homework so well. At the same time in group therapy, Tom became increasingly overconfident that he was cured. He was insistent that with what he had learned in treatment he would never offend again. He was angry with the therapists who challenged this and his response was one of 'I know myself better than you know me.'

He was at that stage in a classic high-risk situation in which he had groomed and had access to a potential victim. He had created situations in which there may not have been other adults present to protect the child, and he was able to justify being dismissive of, and angry with, the therapists who did not 'understand' him. Fortunately, in this case Tom pulled back from the brink and did not abuse the child and returned to treatment which allowed a full exploration of the dangers of relapse.

The men who have completed the programme return every few months for relapse prevention 'top-ups'. The purpose of these meetings is to review their lifestyle and circumstances in the light of what they learned about their individual offence cycle during treatment. Any social or family relationships or employment difficulties experienced by the men are a cause for concern and the implications of their responses to life events regarded as significant in determining the risk of reoffending. Any lapse in attendance for other appointments or at AA or other addiction prevention meetings is also regarded as potentially serious.

The consistent message given to the sex offenders is that they are responsible to ensure that they do not reoffend. They have to make sure that they have learned all the skills and responses which will help them to deal appropriately with any difficulties being experienced. They have to increase their sense of control over their behaviour and recognise warning signs when they occur. Above all they must avoid high-risk situations. GET OUT FAST is the rule.

Notes

INTRODUCTION

1 S. Freud, *Three Essays on the Theory of Sexuality*, 2nd edn (London, Hogarth Press/The Institute of Psychoanalysis, 1905/1953), vol. 8.

2 N. Parton, *Governing the Family: Child Care, Child Protection and the State* (London, Macmillan, 1991).

3 H. Ferguson, 'Child welfare, child protection and the Child Care Act 1991: key issues for policy, practice' in H. Ferguson and P. Kenny (eds.), *On Behalf of the Child: Child Welfare, Child Protection and the Child Care Act 1991* (Dublin, A. & A. Farmar, 1995).

4 K. McKeown and R. Gilligan, 'Child sexual abuse in the Eastern Health Board area of Ireland in 1988: an analysis of 512 confirmed cases', *Economic and Social Review* (1991), 22 (2).

5 R. Gilligan, 'Irish child care services in the 1990s: the Child Care Act and other developments' in M. Hill and J. Aldgate, *Child Care Services – Developments in Law, Policy, Practice and Research* (London, Jessica Kingsley Publishers, 1996).

6 I. Hassall and B. Wood, 'Facing up to child abuse and neglect', paper presented at the 11th International Congress of the International Society for the Prevention of Child Abuse and Neglect (ISPCAN), Dublin, 1996.

I CHILDHOOD EXPERIENCES OF SEXUAL ABUSE

1 S. Sgroi et al., 'A conceptual framework for child sexual abuse' in S. Sgroi (ed.), *Handbook of Clinical Intervention in Child Sexual Abuse* (Lexington, MA, Lexington Books, 1982).

2 J. Whetsell-Mitchell, *Rape of the Innocent: Understanding and Preventing Child Sexual Abuse* (Washington DC, Accelerated Development, Taylor & Francis, 1995).

3 E. Bass and L. Thornton (eds.), *I Have Never Told Anyone: Writings by Women Survivors of Sexual Abuse* (New York, Harper & Row, 1983).

4 NCH Action for Children, *Hearing the Truth. The Importance of Listening to Children who Disclose Sexual Abuse* (London, NCH Action for Children Publications Unit, 1996).

5 N. Roth, *Integrating the Shattered Self: Psychotherapy with Adult Incest Survivors* (Northvale, NJ, Jason Aronson, 1993).

6 G. Adsmead and C. Van Velsen, 'Psychotherapeutic work with victims of trauma' in Christopher Cordess and Murray Cox (eds.), *Forensic Psychotherapy: Crime, Psychodynamics and the Offender Patient*, vol. II, *Mainly Practice*, chapter 19 (London, Jessica Kingsley Publishers, 1996).

7 NCH Action for Children, *Hearing the Truth*.

  8 D. Finkelhor, 'Long-term effects of sexual abuse', paper presented at the
     11th International Congress of the International Society for the
     Prevention of Child Abuse and Neglect (ISPCAN), Dublin, 1996.
  9 NCH Action for Children, *Hearing the Truth*.

2 THE VICTIMS OF SEXUAL ABUSE
  1 F. Briggs, 'Boys – the forgotten victims' in F. Briggs, *From Victim to
     Offender: How Child Sexual Abuse Victims Become Offenders* (Australia, Allen
     & Unwin, 1995).
  2 D. Finkelhor, *A Sourcebook on Child Sexual Abuse* (London, Sage
     Publications, 1986).
  3 Briggs, 'Boys – the forgotten victims'.
  4 Ibid.
  5 M. Lew, *Victims No Longer: Men Recovering from Incest and Other Sexual
     Abuse* (New York, Harper & Row, 1988).
  6 Ibid.
  7 F.J. Pescosolido, 'Sexual abuse of boys by males – theoretical and
     treatment implications', *Treating Abuse Today* (1992), 2 (2).
  8 Lew, *Victims No Longer*.
  9 A.N. Groth and N.J. Birnbaum, *Men Who Rape: The Psychology of the
     Offender* (New York, Plenum Press, 1979).
  10 J.R Conte and V. Schuerman, 'The effects of sexual abuse on children: a
      multi-dimensional view', *Journal of Interpersonal Violence* (1987), 2 (4).
  11 Lew, *Victims No Longer*.
  12 Ibid.
  13 Ibid.
  14 Ibid.

3 ONCE THE ABUSE IS PUBLICLY REVEALED
  1 J. Henry, 'Societal systems trauma to sexually abused children following
     disclosure', paper presented at the 11th International Congress of the
     International Society for the Prevention of Child Abuse and Neglect
     (ISPCAN), Dublin, 1996.
  2 P.C. Alexander, 'Application of attachment theory to the study of sexual
     abuse', *Journal of Consulting and Clinical Psychology* (1992), 60.
  3 D. Finkelhor, 'The trauma of sexual abuse: two models' in G.E. Wyatt
     and G.J. Powell (eds.), *Lasting Effects of Child Sexual Abuse* (Newbury Park,
     CA, Sage Publications, 1988).
  4 North-Western Health Board, *Guidelines for the Investigation and
     Management of Suspected Child Abuse*, 1997.
  5 NCH Action for Children, *Message from Children: Children's Evaluations of the*

Professional Response to Child Sexual Abuse (UK, NCH Action for Children Publications Unit, 1994).

6 Henry, 'Societal systems trauma to sexually abused children following disclosure'.

7 Ibid.

8 NCH Action for Children, *Message from Children*.

9 Ibid.

10 N.I. Ripland, 'The media – help or opposition to victims of incest?', paper presented at the 11th International Congress of the International Society for the Prevention of Child Abuse and Neglect (ISPCAN), Dublin, 1996.

11 E. McAdam and P. Lang, 'Balancing interests', paper presented at the 11th International Congress of the International Society for the Prevention of Child Abuse and Neglect (ISPCAN), Dublin, 1996.

12 Y. Ronew, 'Protection for who and from what? Protection proceedings and the voice of the child at risk', paper presented at the 11th International Congress of the International Society for the Prevention of Child Abuse and Neglect (ISPCAN), Dublin, 1996.

4 FEMALE SEXUAL ABUSERS

1 F. Briggs, *From Victim to Offender: How Child Sexual Abuse Victims Become Offenders* (Australia, Allen & Unwin, 1995).

2 NSPCC, *Voices from Childhood* (London, NSPCC, 1996).

3 A. Bentovim, 'The trauma organised system of working with family violence' in Christopher Cordess and Murray Cox (eds.), *Forensic Psychotherapy: Crime, Psychodynamics and the Offender Patient*, vol. II, *Mainly Practice*, chapter 16 (London, Jessica Kingsley Publishers, 1996).

4 Briggs, *From Victim to Offender*.

5 J. Whetsell-Mitchell, *Rape of the Innocent: Understanding and Preventing Child Sexual Abuse* (Washington DC, Accelerated Development, Taylor & Francis, 1995).

6 Briggs, *From Victim to Offender*.

7 M. Hunter, *Sexually Abused Males,* vol. I, *Prevalence, Impact and Treatment* (Lexington, MA, Free Press, 1990).

8 J. Matthews, R.K. Matthews and K. Speltz, *Female Sexual Offenders: An Exploratory Study* (Orwell, VT, Safer Society Press, 1989).

9 Ibid.

10 L. McCarthy, 'Mother–child incest: characteristics of the offender', *Child Welfare* (1986), 65 (5).

11 C. Lawson, 'Clinical assessment of mother–son sexual abuse', *Clinical Society Work Journal* (1991), 19 (4).

12 Ibid.

13 J.N. Quintano, 'Case profiles of early childhood enema abuse', *Treating Abuse Today* (1992), 2.

14 R.S. Krug, 'Adult male report of childhood sexual abuse by mothers: case descriptions, motivations and long-term consequences', *Child Abuse and Neglect* (1989), 13.

15 J. Goodwin and P. Di Vasto, 'Female homosexuality: a sequel to mother–daughter incest' in J. Goodwin, *Sexual Abuse, Incest Victims and their Families* (Massachusetts, PSG Publishing Company Inc., 1982).

16 Y. Ortiz, J. Pino and J. Goodwin, 'What families say: the dialogue of incest' in J. Goodwin, *Sexual Abuse, Incest Victims and their Families* (Massachusetts, PSG Publishing Company Inc., 1982).

17. E.V. Weldon, 'Contrast in male and female sexual perversions' in Christopher Cordess and Murray Cox (eds.), *Forensic Psychotherapy: Crime, Psychodynamics and the Offender Patient,* vol. II, *Mainly Practice,* chapter 15 (iii) (London, Jessica Kingsley Publishers, 1996).

18 A. Bentovim, 'Why do adults sexually abuse children?', *British Medical Journal* (1993), 307.

19 Weldon, 'Contrast in male and female sexual perversions'.

20 Briggs, *From Victim to Offender.*

21 Ibid.

22 John Waters, 'Statistics of abuse give lie to the myth of good mother', *Irish Times,* 11 November 1997.

23 Medb Ruane, 'Women also capable of sex abuse', *Irish Times,* 28 February 1998.

24 *Irish Times,* 4 May 1998.

25 *Irish Times,* 12 February 1998.

5 WHY ALL ABUSERS ARE NOT THE SAME

1 J. Whetsell-Mitchell, *Rape of the Innocent: Understanding and Preventing Child Sexual Abuse* (Washington DC, Accelerated Development, Taylor & Francis, 1995).

2 A.N. Groth and N.J. Birnbaum, *Men Who Rape: The Psychology of the Offender* (New York, Plenum Press, 1979).

3 L. Kelly, 'Weasel words – paedophiles and the abuse cycle', *NOTA News* (June 1997), 22.

4 R. Wyre, *Working with Sex Abuse: Understanding Sex Offending* (Oxford, Perry Publications, 1987).

5 K. Wallis, 'Perspectives of child molesters' in F. Briggs, *From Victim to Offender: How Child Sexual Abuse Victims Become Offenders* (Australia, Allen & Unwin, 1995).

6. H.E. Barbaree, W.L. Marshall and J. McCormick, 'The development of

deviant sexual behaviour among adolescents and its implications for prevention and treatment', *Irish Journal of Psychology* (1998), 19 (1).

7 G.E. Davis and M. Leitenberg, 'Adolescent sex offenders', *Psychological Bulletin* (1987), 101.

8 G. O'Reilly and A. Carr, 'Child abuse in Ireland: a synthesis of two studies' (unpublished), discussed in D. Sheerin, 'Legal options in Ireland for getting adolescent sex offenders into treatment and keeping them there', *Irish Journal of Psychology* (1998), 19 (1).

9 H.E. Barbaree, S.M. Hudson and M.C. Seto, 'Sexual abuse in society: the role of the juvenile offender' in H.E. Barbaree, W.L. Marshall and S.M. Hudson (eds.), *The Juvenile Sex Offender* (New York, Guilford Press, 1993).

10 Whetsell-Mitchell, *Rape of the Innocent*.

11 W.D. Pithers, A. Gray, A. Busconi and P. Houshens, 'Five empirically derived subtypes of children with sexual behaviour problems: characteristics potentially related to juvenile delinquency and adult criminality', *Irish Journal of Psychology* (1998), 19 (1).

12 Barbaree, Marshall and McCormick, 'The development of deviant sexual behaviour among adolescents and its implications for prevention and treatment'.

13 J.V. Becker, 'The assessment of adolescent perpetrators of childhood sexual abuse', *Irish Journal of Psychology* (1998), 19 (1).

14 G. O'Reilly, A. Sheridan, A. Carr, J. Cherry, K. Donohue, K. McGrath, S. Phelan, M. Tallon and K. O'Reilly, 'A descriptive study of adolescent sexual offenders in an Irish community-based treatment programme', *Irish Journal of Psychology* (1998), 19 (1).

15 J. Kobayashi, B.D. Sales, J.V. Becker, A.J. Figueredo and M.S. Kaplan, 'Perceived parental deviance, parent–child bonding, child abuse, child sexual aggression', *Sexual Abuse: A Journal of Research and Treatment* (1995), 7.

16 Pithers, Gray, Busconi and Houshens, 'Five empirically derived subtypes of children with sexual behaviour problems'.

6 THE PSYCHOLOGICAL PERSPECTIVES

1 R. Wyre, *Working with Sex Abuse: Understanding Sex Offending* (Oxford, Perry Publications, 1987).

2 S. Freud, *Three Contributions to the Theory of Sex*, 4th edn (New York, Nervous and Mental Disease Monographs, 1948).

3 M. Fraser, *The Death of Narcissus* (London, Secker & Warburg, 1976).

4 W. Kraemer, *The Forbidden Love: The Normal and Abnormal Love of Children* (London, Sheldon Press, 1976).

5 K. Howells, 'Adult sexual interest in children: considerations relevant to theories of aetiology' in M. Cook and K. Howells (eds.), *Adult Sexual Interest in Children* (London, Academic Press, 1981).

6 H. Eldridge, *The Faithful Foundation, Assessment and Therapy Relapse Prevention Programme for Adult Male Sex Abusers* (UK, Faithful Foundation, 1992).

7 A. Bentovim, 'The trauma organised system of working with family violence' in Christopher Cordess and Murray Cox (eds.), *Forensic Psychotherapy: Crime, Psychodynamics and the Offender Patient*, vol. II, *Mainly Practice*, chapter 16 (London, Jessica Kingsley Publishers, 1996).

8 A. Miller, *For Your Own Good: The Roots of Violence in Child Rearing* (London, Virago Press, 1987).

9 J. Bowlby, *Attachment and Loss,* vol. I, *Attachment* (London, Hogarth Press, 1969).

10 W.L. Marshall, 'The role of attachment, intimacy and loneliness in the aetiology and maintenance of sexual offending', *Sexual and Marital Therapy* (1993), 8.

11 K. Bartholomew, 'From childhood to adult relationships, attachment theory and research' in S. Duck (ed.), *Learning about Relationships* (Newbury Park, CA, Sage Publications, 1993).

12 H.E. Barbaree, W.L. Marshall and J. McCormick, 'The development of deviant sexual behaviour among adolescents and its implications for prevention and treatment', *Irish Journal of Psychology* (1998), 19 (1).

13 T. Ward, S. Hudson and W.L. Marshall, 'Attachment style in sex offenders: a preliminary study', *Journal of Sex Research* (1996), 33.

14 W.L. Marshall, D. Anderson and F. Champagne, 'Self-esteem and its relationship to sexual offending', *Psychology, Crime and Law* (1996), 3.

15 K.M. Wallis, 'Perspectives on child molesters' in F. Briggs, *From Victim to Offender: How Child Sexual Abuse Victims Become Offenders* (Australia, Allen & Unwin, 1995).

16 K. Freund, 'Assessment of paedophilia' in M. Cook and K. Howells (eds.), *Adult Sexual Interest in Children* (London, Academic Press, 1981).

17 Wyre, *Working with Sex Abuse*.

18 D. Finkelhor and S. Arajis, *Explanations of Paedophilia: A Four-track Mode*, University of New Hampshire Family Violence Research Program, 1983.

19 A. Bentovim, 'Family systemic approach to work with young sex offenders', *Irish Journal of Psychology* (1998), 19 (1).

20 J.L. Herman and L. Hirschman, *Father–Daughter Incest* (Cambridge, MA and London, Harvard University Press, 1981).

21 Bentovim, 'The trauma organised system of working with family violence'.

22 Ibid.

23 C.A. Courtois, *Healing the Incest Wound: Adult Survivors in Therapy* (New York, W.W. Norton, 1988).

24 R. Fredrickson, 'The family system: untold lies' in R. Fredrickson, *Repressed Memories: A Journey to Recovery from Sexual Abuse* (New York, Simon & Schuster, 1992).

25 Bentovim, 'The trauma organised system of working with family violence'.

26 Bentovim, 'Family systemic approach to work with young sex offenders'.

7 SEXUAL ABUSE AND THE MEDIA

1 John Horgan, 'Court ban puts media motive in spotlight', *Irish Times*, 7 February 1997.

2 Fintan O'Toole, 'Facing up to facts of paedophilia and taking action', *Irish Times*, 23 August 1996.

8 LIVING WITH THE EXPERIENCE OF SEXUAL ABUSE

1 M. Hancock and K. Burton Mains, *Child Sexual Abuse: A Hope for Healing* (Surrey, Highland Books, 1988).

2 D. Finkelhor, 'Long-term effects of sexual abuse', paper presented at the 11th International Congress of the International Society for the Prevention of Child Abuse and Neglect (ISPCAN), Dublin, 1996.

3 D. Finkelhor, 'The victimisation of children: a developmental perspective', *American Journal of Orthopsychiatry* (April 1995), 65 (2).

4 L.J. Kirby, J. Cnu and D.L. Dill, 'Correlates of disassociative symptomatology in patients with physical and sexual abuse histories', *Comprehensive Psychiatry* (1993), 34 (4).

5 P.M. Cole and F.W. Putnam, 'Effect of incest on self and social functioning: a developmental psychopathology perspective', *Journal of Consulting and Clinical Psychology* (1992), 60.

6 T.W. Wind and L. Silvern, 'Parenting and family stress as mediators of the long-term effects of child abuse', *Child Abuse and Neglect* (1994), 18.

7 S. Spaccerell, 'Stress appraisal and coping in child sexual abuse: a theoretical and empirical review', *Psychological Bulletin* (1994), 116.

8 P.C. Alexander, 'Application of attachment theory to the study of sexual abuse', *Journal of Consulting and Clinical Psychology* (1992), 60.

9 Kirby, Cnu and Dill, 'Correlates of disassociative symptomatology in patients with physical and sexual abuse histories'.

10 M.P. Celeno, 'A developmental model of victims: internal attributions of responsibility for sexual abuse', *Journal of Interpersonal Violence* (1992), 7.

11 Cole and Putnam, 'Effect of incest on self and social functioning'.

12 K.A. Kendall-Tackett, L.M. Williams and D. Finkelhor, 'Impact of sexual abuse on children: a review and synthesis of recent empirical studies', *Psychological Bulletin* (1993), 113 (1).

13 B. Watkins and A. Bentovim, 'The sexual abuse of male children and adolescents: a review of current research', *Journal of Child Psychology and Psychiatry and Allied Disciplines* (1992), 33 (1).

14 W.N. Friedrich et al., 'Child sexual abuse behaviour inventory: normative and clinical comparisons', *Psychological Assessment* (1992), 4.

15 M. Rutter, 'Resilience in the face of adversity: protective factors and resistance to psychiatric disorder', *British Journal of Psychiatry* (1985), 147.

16 M. Rutter, 'Psychosocial resilience and protective mechanisms', *American Journal of Orthopsychiatry* (1987), 57.

17 Finkelhor, 'Long-term effects of sexual abuse'.

18 F.W. Putnam and P.K. Trickett, 'Child sexual abuse: a model of chronic trauma' in J.E. Dreiss, J.E. Richters and M. Radke-Yarrow (eds.), *Children and Violence* (New York, Guilford Press, 1993).

19 J.M. Ussher and C. Dewberry, 'The nature and long-term effects of childhood sexual abuse: a survey of adult women survivors in Britain', *British Journal of Clinical Psychology* (1995), 34.

20 Finkelhor, 'Long-term effects of sexual abuse'.

21 Ibid.

22 Ussher and Dewberry, 'The nature and long-term effects of childhood sexual abuse'.

23 C.E. Hamilton and K.D. Browne, 'The repeat victimisation of children: should the concept be revised?', *Journal of Aggression and Violent Behaviour* (1997), 2.

24 Finkelhor, 'Long-term effects of sexual abuse'.

25 Hancock and Burton Mains, *Child Sexual Abuse*.

26 Finkelhor, 'Long-term effects of sexual abuse'.

27 Hancock and Burton Mains, *Child Sexual Abuse*.

28 Finkelhor, 'Long-term effects of sexual abuse'.

29 C. Pinkola Estes, *Women Who Run with the Wolves: Contacting the Power of the Wild Women* (London, Rider, 1992).

9 A RESPONSIBLE APPROACH TO LESSENING ABUSE

 1 V. Sinason, 'From abused to abuser' in Christopher Cordess and Murray Cox (eds.), *Forensic Psychotherapy: Crime, Psychodynamics and the Offender Patient*, vol. II, *Mainly Practice* (London, Jessica Kingsley Publishers, 1996).

 2 Theresa Judge, 'Do sex-fuelled teen mags go too far?', *Irish Times*, 9 September 1997.

 3 M.E. Ford and J.A. Linney, 'Comparative analysis of juvenile sexual

offenders: violent non-sexual offenders and status offenders', *Journal of Interpersonal Violence* (1995), 10.

4 NSPCC, *Voices from Childhood* (London, NSPCC, 1996).

5 Barnardo's, *Children First* (Dublin, Barnardo's, 1997).

10   A CURE FOR SEX OFFENDING?

1 P. O'Mahony, *Criminal Chaos: Seven Crises in Irish Criminal Jusice* (Dublin, Round Hall, Sweet & Maxwell, 1996).

2 P. Murphy, 'A therapeutic programme for imprisoned sex offenders: progress to date and issues for the future', *Irish Journal of Psychology* (1998), 19 (1).

3 NOTA Conference (June 1995), 'Can there be justice for children in the criminal justice system?', *NOTA News* (April 1996), 17.

4 C.R. Hollins, 'Training for residential work with young offenders: structure and content', *Issues in Criminology and Legal Psychology* (1991), 2.

5 T. Gooch, 'Why not measure the obvious?', *NOTA News* (June 1996), 18.

CONCLUSION

1 C.R. Hollins, 'Training for residential work with young offenders: structure and content', *Issues in Criminology and Legal Psychology* (1991), 2.

2 P. Murphy, 'A therapeutic programme for imprisoned sex offenders: progress to date and issues for the future', *Irish Journal of Psychology* (1998), 19 (1).

3 Department of Education, *Stay Safe Programme* (Dublin, Child Abuse Prevention Programme, 1991).

4 Department of Education, *Relationships and Sexuality Education* (Dublin, 1997).

5 N.I. Ripland, 'The media – help or opposition to victims of incest?', paper presented at the 11th International Congress of the International Society for the Prevention of Child Abuse and Neglect (ISPCAN), Dublin, 1996.

APPENDIX

1 P. Kenny, 'The Child Care Act 1991 and the social context of child protection' in H. Ferguson and P. Kenny (eds.), *On Behalf of the Child: Child Welfare, Child Protection and the Child Care Act 1991* (Dublin, A. & A. Farmar, 1995).

2 T. McCormack, 'Approaches to family and community education' in H. Ferguson and P. Kenny (eds.), *On Behalf of the Child: Child Welfare, Child Protection and the Child Care Act 1991* (Dublin, A. & A. Farmar, 1995).

3 R. Wyre, *Working with Sex Abuse: Understanding Sex Offending* (Oxford, Perry Publications, 1987).

4 The Kia Marama Programme for Sexual Offenders, Rolleston Prison, New Zealand.

5 E. McAdam and P. Lang, 'Developing new moral order with perpetrators', paper presented at the 11th International Congress of the International Society for the Prevention of Child Abuse and Neglect (ISPCAN), Dublin, 1996.

6 F.M. Knopp, *Retraining Adult Sex Offenders – Methods and Models* (Orwell, VT, Safer Society Press, 1984).

7 *Kia Marama Relapse Prevention Workbook*, Special Treatment Unit, Rolleston Prison, New Zealand.

Index